Build your own *Custom*

WORKBENCH

Mark Corke

POPULAR WOODWORKING BOOKS
CINCINNATI, OHIO
www.popularwoodworking.com

READ THIS IMPORTANT SAFETY NOTICE

To prevent accidents, keep safety in mind while you work. Use the safety guards installed on power equipment; they are for your protection. When working on power equipment, keep fingers away from saw blades, wear safety goggles to prevent injuries from flying wood chips and sawdust, wear headphones to protect your hearing, and consider installing a dust vacuum to reduce the amount of airborne sawdust in your woodshop. Don't wear loose clothing, such as neckties or shirts with loose sleeves, or jewelry, such as rings, necklaces or bracelets, when working on power equipment. Tie back long hair to prevent it from getting caught in your equipment. People who are sensitive to certain chemicals should check the chemical content of any product before using it. The authors and editors who compiled this book have tried to make the contents as accurate and correct as possible. Plans, illustrations, photographs and text have been carefully checked. All instructions, plans and projects should be carefully read, studied and understood before beginning construction. In some photos, power tool guards have been removed to more clearly show the operation being demonstrated. Always use all safety guards and attachments that come with your power tools. Due to the variability of local conditions, construction materials, skill levels, etc., neither the author nor Popular Woodworking Books assumes any responsibility for any accidents, injuries, damages or other losses incurred resulting from the material presented in this book. Prices listed for supplies and equipment were current at the time of publication and are subject to change. Glass shelving should have all edges polished and must be tempered. Untempered glass shelves may shatter and can cause serious bodily injury. Tempered shelves are very strong and if they break will just crumble, minimizing personal injury.

Build Your Own Custom Workbench. Copyright © 2003 by Mark Corke. Printed in Singapore. All rights reserved. No part of this book may be reproduced in any form or by any electronic or mechanical means including information storage and retrieval systems without permission in writing from the publisher, except by a reviewer, who may quote brief passages in a review. Published by Popular Woodworking Books, an imprint of F&W Publications, Inc., 4700 East Galbraith Road, Cincinnati, Ohio, 45236. First edition.

Visit our Web site at www.popularwoodworking.com for information on more resources for woodworkers.

Other fine Popular Woodworking Books are available from your local bookstore or direct from the publisher.

07   06   05   04   03   5   4   3   2   1

Library of Congress Cataloging-in-Publication Data

Corke, Mark.
   Build your own custom workbench / by Mark Corke.
     p. cm.
   Includes index.
   ISBN 1-55870-678-x (alk. paper)
   1. Workbenches--Design and construction. 2. Woodwork--Equipment and supplies--Design and construction. I. Title.
  TT197.5.W6C67 2003
  684'.08--dc21

             2003048214

Acquisitions editor: Jim Stack
Edited by Jennifer Ziegler
Designed by Lisa Buchanan
Production coordinated by Mark Griffin
Layout artist: Matthew DeRhodes
Technical illustrations by Melanie Powell

METRIC CONVERSION CHART

to convert	to	multiply by
Inches	Centimeters	2.54
Centimeters	Inches	0.4
Feet	Centimeters	30.5
Centimeters	Feet	0.03
Yards	Meters	0.9
Meters	Yards	1.1
Sq. Inches	Sq. Centimeters	6.45
Sq. Centimeters	Sq. Inches	0.16
Sq. Feet	Sq. Meters	0.09
Sq. Meters	Sq. Feet	10.8
Sq. Yards	Sq. Meters	0.8
Sq. Meters	Sq. Yards	1.2
Pounds	Kilograms	0.45
Kilograms	Pounds	2.2
Ounces	Grams	28.4
Grams	Ounces	0.035

To my wife, Rita, who has always had faith in my work in all its aspects; photo assistant, woodworking helper and sailing mate. To her I am eternally grateful. With every book that I write, photo that I take or woodworking project that I undertake, she, more than anyone, has given me the encouragement to see it through. For that I thank her from the bottom of my heart.

To my son, Sam, who has started to pick up tools and experience the joys of woodworking.

Finally to my Mum and Dad, May and Goff, who have read just about everything that I have ever written and have always encouraged me in everything I have done in my lifetime.

ABOUT THE AUTHOR

Born in England, Mark Corke became interested in woodworking at an early age, when he helped his dad remodel the back of the house in London. At school, when other students were making table lamps and towel holders in woodworking class, Mark built a boat, the first of many. After leaving school, he went to college to study journalism and photography, and eventually ended up working for the BBC as an editor. All the while he was pursuing a strong interest in spare-time woodworking. After leaving the BBC he became technical editor of Britain's best-selling *Good Woodworking* magazine, a position he held for five years. Mark has regularly appeared on TV and radio both as a host and a woodworking expert.

After moving to the United States with his wife, he settled on the Connecticut shore, where he pursues his career as a freelance writer and photographer. He still makes and sails home-built boats in his spare time.

ACKNOWLEDGEMENTS

I would like to extend my thanks to those who helped in the production of this book, especially Jim Stack and Julia Groh of F&W. Without them this book would never have seen the light of day.

I would also like to thank Barry Pope, product manager of American Tool, and Sil Argentin and John Roberts of Bosch power tools for their invaluable help with products and advice.

Thanks and appreciation to Phil Davy of *Good Woodworking* magazine who continues to be a source of inspiration, humor and ideas. He showed me that woodworking and doughnuts do go together.

Finally I would like to thank all those people who have given me encouragement in my woodworking and professional life, especially Ron Penfound, my school woodworking teacher who did so much to give me an interest in woodworking and wooden boats.

table of contents

INTRODUCTION

When I first started to think about this book, I wondered if I could find enough material to fill it. After all, everybody knows what workbenches are. Is a book really necessary? But the more I thought about it, the more I realized that the workbench demanded a book all to itself. Far from wondering what I would put in, I wondered what I should leave out.

Those of us who spend any time at all in the workshop do not give a second thought to the workbench, yet it is the focus of much of the activity. Imagine how hard it would be to work without one. This book goes some way to redress the balance in favor of the humble workbench. None of the projects in this book are particularly difficult, and some are decidedly simple, but they all perform their required function, thus making your woodworking more enjoyable.

There are probably as many different workbench designs as there are woodworkers. We are all unique, but these designs suit me well, as I am sure they will you, too. As you work through the book, feel free to alter designs to suit your preferences and tastes. Happy woodworking.

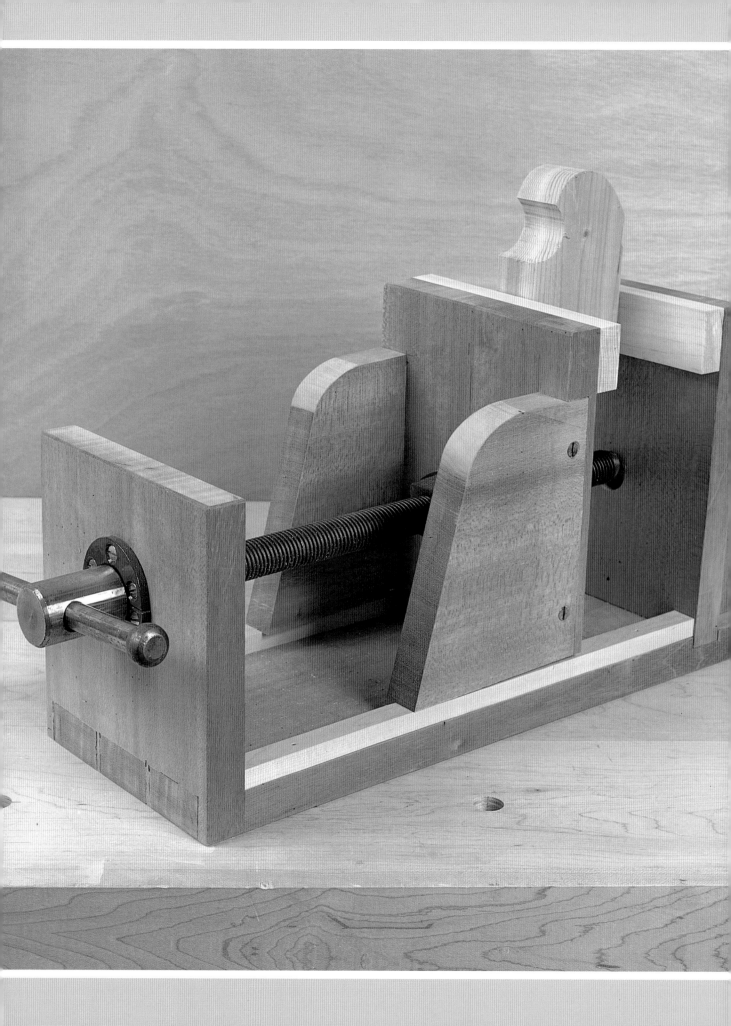

carver's VICE

One of my passions is making canoe paddles and other carvings from time to time. Holding the work in a standard bench vise is far from ideal, as it falls short on several counts. Namely, it is too low and will not hold circular work easily. Needing to address these and other points, I designed and built this carver's vise, sometimes called carver's chops, to enable me to work on paddles and other shaped work more easily. A friend of mine who does a lot of carving has no need of a proper workbench, and uses a carver's vise very similar to this all the time.

This project is inexpensive and quick to make, and the most expensive part is the bench screw. Mine utilizes the screw available from Record, and constructional details and dimensions suit this, but you should use any manufacturer's screw that is readily available. You will then need to adjust the dimensions slightly to take this into account.

Construction is simple, and I built my vise in a day, but whatever you do, don't rush. Building this vise is a good chance to show off your cabinetmaking skills. Sloppy joinery will prevent the jaws from coming together correctly, and could prevent the sliding jaw from having a smooth action.

A hole drilled through the base enables the long bolt to be inserted through a dog hole in the bench, where a large nut and washer under the bench hold the vise securely and enable it to be turned to present the work at a suitable angle. Alternatively, or for the occasional user, you can just do as I do and hold it in the main work vise or clamp it to the bench top with a C-clamp.

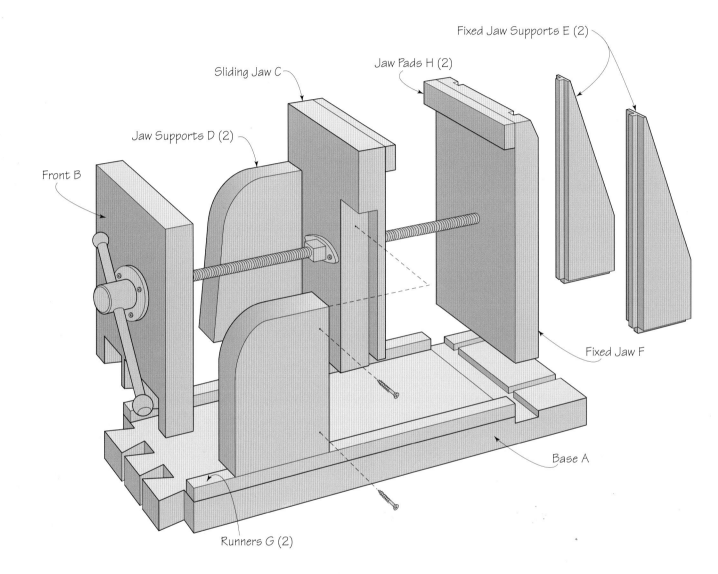

Fixed Jaw Supports E (2)

Jaw Pads H (2)

Sliding Jaw C

Jaw Supports D (2)

Front B

Fixed Jaw F

Base A

Runners G (2)

inches (millimeters)

REFERENCE	QUANTITY	PART	STOCK	THICKNESS	(mm)	WIDTH	(mm)	LENGTH	(mm)	COMMENTS
A	1	base	mahogany	$1\frac{1}{4}$	(32)	$7\frac{1}{4}$	(184)	21	(533)	
B	1	front	mahogany	$1\frac{1}{4}$	(32)	$7\frac{1}{4}$	(184)	8	(203)	
C	1	sliding jaw	mahogany	$1\frac{1}{4}$	(32)	$7\frac{1}{4}$	(184)	$9\frac{1}{2}$	(242)	
D	2	jaw supports	mahogany	$1\frac{1}{4}$	(32)	$5\frac{1}{2}$	(140)	7	(178)	for sliding jaw
E	1	fixed jaw	mahogany	$1\frac{1}{4}$	(32)	$7\frac{1}{4}$	(184)	$9\frac{7}{8}$	(251)	
F	2	fixed jaw supports	mahogany	$1\frac{1}{4}$	(32)	3	(76)	$8\frac{1}{2}$	(216)	for fixed jaw
G	2	runners	maple	$\frac{3}{4}$	(19)	$\frac{1}{2}$	(13)	16	(406)	
H	2	jaw pads	pine	$\frac{3}{4}$	(19)	$1\frac{1}{2}$	(38)	$7\frac{1}{4}$	(184)	leather is an alternative

HARDWARE

Wood glue
Bench screw — Record part #165/18
8   $1\frac{1}{4}$" × $\frac{1}{4}$" (32mm × 6mm) Countersunk nuts and bolts
1   $1\frac{1}{2}$" (38mm) No. 10 wood screws
2d Finish nails

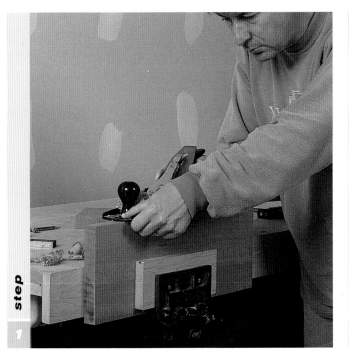

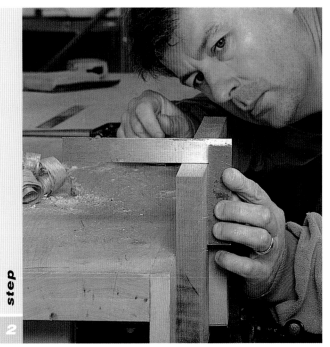

This project is as much a piece of cabinetmaking as it is a vise. I planed all the parts with a sharp plane to remove any surface imperfections and ripple left from the planer.

Check all the measurements with a square to make sure that everything is perfect. Warped wood will make the completed vise twist and prevent it from sliding correctly.

Carefully set out the dovetails. I used three large ones, but you could use smaller tails if you prefer. Machine-cut dovetails are not really appropriate, as many of them are too small to withstand the pressure to which they will be subjected on the carver's vise. Note, too, that the tails are cut on the base and the pins on the front. If you cut them the wrong way around, the pressure will force them apart.

Cut down to the shoulder line with a dovetail saw, then chop out the waste with a suitably sized chisel. Clamp the work with some scrap to prevent damage to the bench. The top piece of wood is clamped in line with the dovetail shoulders and acts as a guide for the chisel.

I prefer to cut out most of the waste from between the pins with a coping saw, leaving about $^1/_8$" to cut back to the line with the chisel.

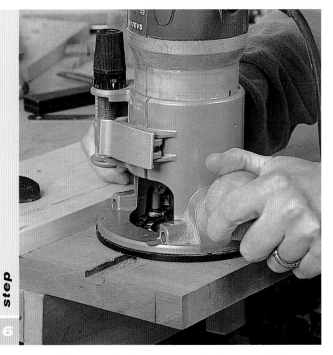

step 6

Rout a dado across the base to accept the bottom of the fixed jaw.

step 7

Use a $1^{1}/_{4}$" Forstner bit to drill the hole through the front to allow the bench screw to pass through. To find the position for the hole, put a mark on the center line $4^{1}/_{2}$" up from the shoulder line.

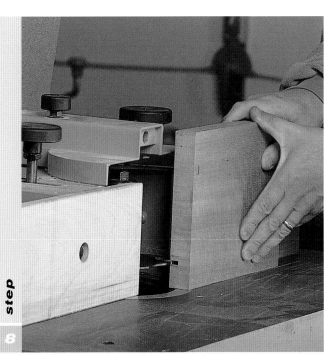

step 8

The fixed jaw is supported by two triangular pieces that are tongued into the back. Cut a groove $^{3}/_{8}$" wide by $^{1}/_{2}$" deep, 1" in from either side. I used a slotting cutter in the shaper, but a router and suitable cutter works just fine, too.

step 9

After cutting a groove on a shaper, cut a triangular shape. Clean it up with a sharp plane.

Fit the runners, making sure that they are parallel. Do not put any glue on these, but simply pin them into position with three or four panel pins; then, if they wear, they can easily be replaced.

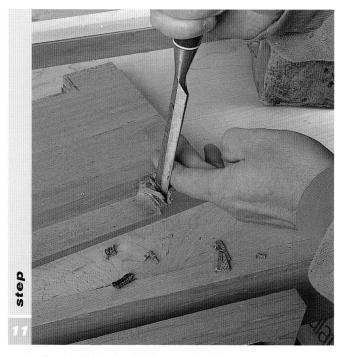

Make the sliding jaw by first cutting the rabbets for the support pieces. Cut these with a router $1\frac{1}{4}$" wide and $\frac{7}{8}$" deep, stopping $1\frac{3}{4}$" from the top. Square off the corner left by the router with a sharp chisel.

Cut the rounded profile of the supports on the band saw and clean them up with a plane and sandpaper. Cut one and use it as a template to make an exact copy, thus forming an identical pair.

Glue and screw the jaw supports into place using brass screws, after you have drilled for the bench screw nut. As with the front, drill the hole with a $1\frac{1}{4}$" Forstner bit, $4\frac{1}{2}$" up from the bottom. Attach the vise nut with nuts and bolts, not wood screws.

step 14

Temporarily assemble the vise with the bench screw in place, and mark the position of the bolts with a bradawl.

step 15

Drill clearance holes for the bolts that hold the retaining collar in position. Then refit the screw, and bolt the retaining collar into position.

step 16

Fit the jaw pads. I used softwood, but an alternative would be some thick leather.

step 17

Finally, rub a little candle wax on the runners to make the jaw slide easily.

collapsible WORKBENCH

I built this bench for my neighbor Tom, who wanted somewhere to do the odd bit of woodworking, but who lacked the space and the finances for anything bigger.

I built the bench in a day for less than $150, but even so, it has all the necessary attributes of a serious workbench. Best of all, the bench breaks down into four sections for easy storage and handling. The legs fit inside the frame under the top, and the shelf comes off and can be stored separately if space is really tight. The whole bench can fit under a single bed, so it could conceivably be used in an apartment.

To save time, the bench top is a solid-core door, which both has the necessary mass to absorb hammer blows and is perfectly flat, making it ideal for the main work surface.

All the lumber was bought at a home center to finished dimensions, so all that was necessary was to cut it to length and join the parts together.

I joined some parts with dowel joints, which are both quick and strong. An alternate method would be to fit blocks into the corners and screw the parts into them.

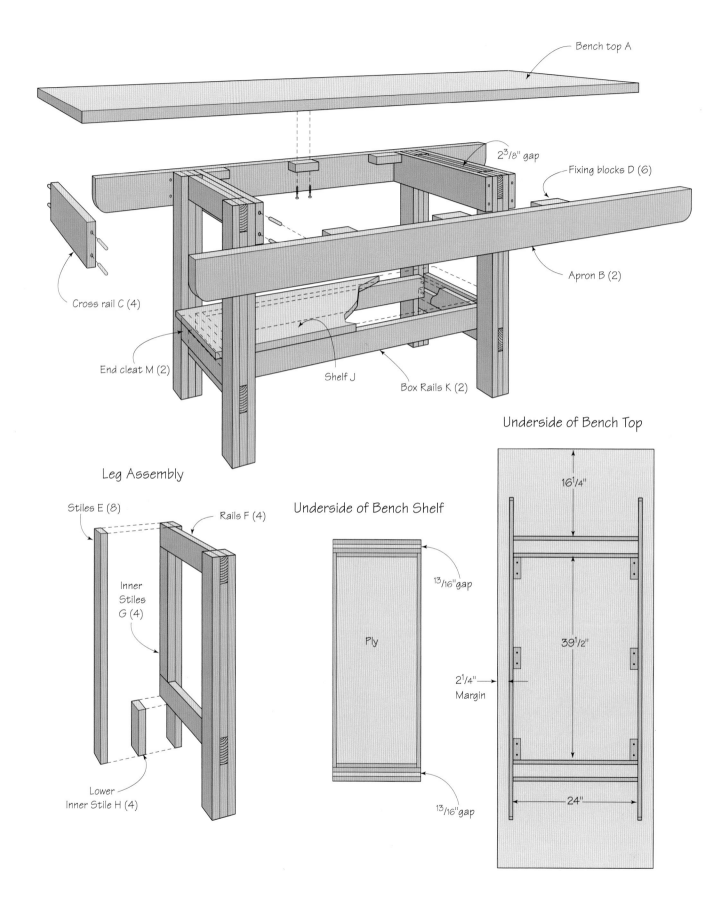

Bench top A

2³⁄₈" gap

Fixing blocks D (6)

Apron B (2)

Cross rail C (4)

End cleat M (2)

Shelf J

Box Rails K (2)

Underside of Bench Top

Leg Assembly

Stiles E (8)

Rails F (4)

Inner Stiles G (4)

Underside of Bench Shelf

Ply

¹³⁄₁₆"gap

16¹⁄₄"

39¹⁄₂"

2¹⁄₄" Margin

24"

Lower Inner Stile H (4)

¹³⁄₁₆"gap

inches (millimeters)

REFERENCE	QUANTITY	PART	STOCK	THICKNESS	(mm)	WIDTH	(mm)	LENGTH	(mm)	COMMENTS
Bench top										
A	1	bench top	solid-core door	$1^{3}/_{8}$	(35)	30	(762)	80	(2032)	
B	2	aprons	pine	$^{3}/_{4}$	(19)	$5^{1}/_{2}$	(140)	60	(1524)	rounded on ends
C	4	cross rails	pine	$^{3}/_{4}$	(19)	$5^{1}/_{2}$	(140)	24	(610)	
D	6	fixing blocks	pine	$1^{1}/_{2}$	(38)	$1^{1}/_{2}$	(38)	4	(102)	
Legs										
E	8	stiles	pine	$^{3}/_{4}$	(19)	$3^{1}/_{2}$	(89)	35	(889)	forms the outer laminations
F	4	rails	pine	$^{3}/_{4}$	(19)	$3^{1}/_{2}$	(89)	24	(610)	
G	4	inner stiles	pine	$^{3}/_{4}$	(19)	$3^{1}/_{2}$	(89)	$21^{1}/_{2}$	(546)	
H	4	lower inner stiles	pine	$^{3}/_{4}$	(19)	$3^{1}/_{2}$	(89)	$6^{7}/_{8}$	(174)	
Tool shelf										
J	1	shelf	plywood	$^{3}/_{4}$	(19)	$16^{7}/_{8}$	(428)	48	(1219)	
K	2	box rails	pine	$^{3}/_{4}$	(19)	$3^{1}/_{2}$	(89)	$42^{7}/_{8}$	(1089)	
L	2	cross rails	pine	$^{3}/_{4}$	(19)	$3^{1}/_{2}$	(89)	$15^{1}/_{4}$	(387)	
M	2	end cleats	pine	$^{3}/_{4}$	(19)	$3^{1}/_{2}$	(89)	$16^{7}/_{8}$	(428)	

HARDWARE

Wood glue
$2^{1}/_{2}$" (64mm) No. 8 screws
2" (51mm) No. 8 screws
$1^{1}/_{2}$" (38mm) No. 8 screws
$^{5}/_{16}$" (8mm) Dowels
Finishing nails
Vise

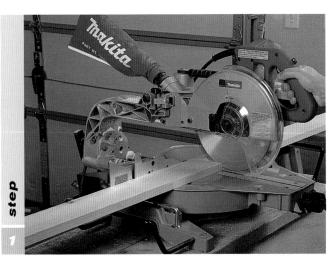

step 1

Start by cutting all the sections of solid lumber to length. The finished bench is just over 3' high. Adjust the height of the legs if this is too low or too high for you.

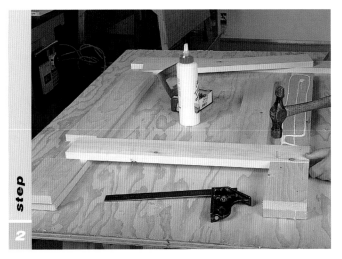

step 2

Glue up the frames for the leg assemblies. All the sections are laminated, so they tend to slide about when they have glue on them. Use one or two strategically placed finishing nails to stop this.

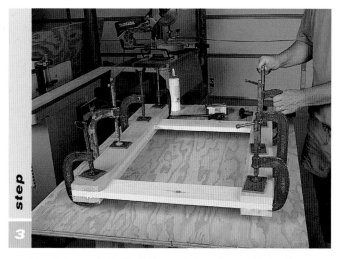

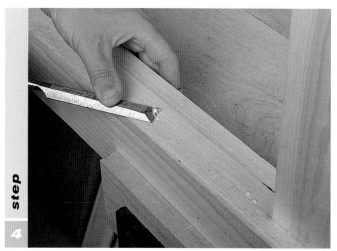

Use C-clamps to hold all the parts together until the glue sets. To avoid marring the wood, use some scraps of hardwood or thin lumber under the clamps.

I know that many people use a damp cloth for wiping off the glue that squeezes out of the joints. A technique that I often use is to wait until the glue is just starting to get sticky and peel it off with a sharp chisel. This has the advantage over the rag method in that it does not make the surrounding wood damp and raise the grain.

After the glue has completely set, plane the outside surfaces of the legs until they are smooth and flat. Plane in from the top to avoid tearing out the grain on the top rail.

Smooth all sharp corners with sandpaper and put the completed legs aside while you work on the other bench parts.

I drew out a 2$^{1}/_{2}$" radius on the ends of the aprons. This looks neat and removes the sharp corners from under the bench, preventing accidents. Compasses are ideal, but you can simply draw around a suitably sized paint can.

Cut to the line with a jigsaw. I could have cut out the curve on the band saw, but the 5' length makes holding the lumber rather difficult.

Use a disc sander or handheld belt sander to clean up the cut edges.

I used $^5/_{16}$" dowels to join the cross rails to the apron. Two dowels are sufficient to give a good joint. A doweling jig ensures that the dowels are perfectly aligned and vertical.

This shot shows the marking for the dowels in the aprons. Square a line $6^5/_{18}$" from each end. Mark the centers of the dowels $1^1/_2$" from each edge. Measure a further $3^1/_8$" from the first line, square a second line and mark for the second set of dowels. Do this on the inside face of each end of the two apron pieces. Accuracy is critical here. If the lines are too far apart, the legs will be a sloppy fit. If the lines are too close, the legs will either be too tight or not fit at all.

Drill the holes for the dowels. Be careful not to drill through the face. Glue the dowels in place with wood glue.

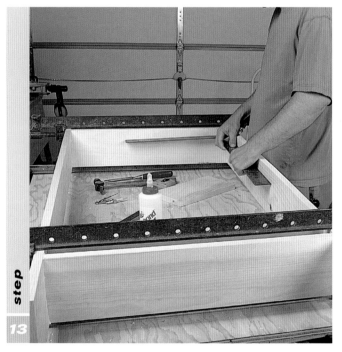

Put glue onto the ends of the cross rails and tap all the parts together. Clamp the bench frame and check to make sure that it is square before letting the glue set.

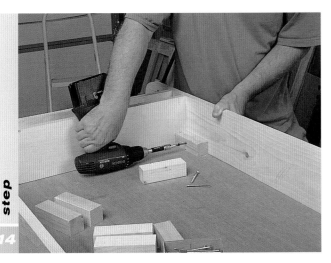

When the glue is dry, remove the clamps and screw the frame to the underside of the door blank that forms the bench top. Make sure that the frame is centered correctly, then fix the top to the frame with the fixing blocks. Use 2¹/₂" screws through the blocks into the top, but use only 2" screws into the frame to avoid drilling through the face.

Make the box frame for the shelf before gluing, and screw it to the plywood shelf using 1¹/₂" No. 8 screws. I joined the frame at the corners with dowels in the same way that I joined the apron frame together.

Using 1¹/₂" No. 6 screws, glue and screw on the end cleats using a scrap of 3¹/₂" × ³/₄" lumber as a spacer. With the cleat in place, the spacer should slide in and out freely without being sloppy.

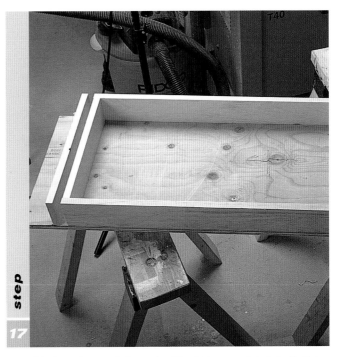

This is a picture of the underside of the completed shelf. Note that the plywood has one good face. The side toward the camera with all the knots will be hidden from view when the bench is in use. To use the bench, slide the leg assemblies between the cross rails in the top frame. Stand the bench up and slide the shelf assembly over the lower leg rails.

fold-down WORKBENCH

This bench was designed for the smaller shop or for a woodworker for whom the garage doubles as a workshop. When folded, it takes up little room, yet is large and sturdy enough to offer good, flat bench space for the seasoned woodworker. The integral work light means that you won't be working in your own shadow, and the bench offers ample storage for tools and workshop supplies. I made mine with a couple of drawers, but these could be omitted and some small doors installed instead, onto which tool racks could be attached.

Construction is straightforward, and it should be possible to complete the bench in one weekend. There are no difficult joints, although a router is used to cut the housings and rabbets for the shelves and back. Almost all the components are made from ¾"-thick plywood, which is available at the local lum-

beryard or home center, but you could use better plywood if the bench is to be installed inside an apartment or will be on display.

Even if you build another bench, this fold-down version will still come in handy, as it could easily be converted into a woodworker's sharpening station or even a potting bench for a gardener.

The dimensions shown give a bench height of 3', which suits my 5'10" stature, but you can easily alter the height of the legs to suit yourself.

One final note. The bench is heavy, which helps keep vibration to a minimum, but this also means that it will require the bench to be tightly secured to the wall.

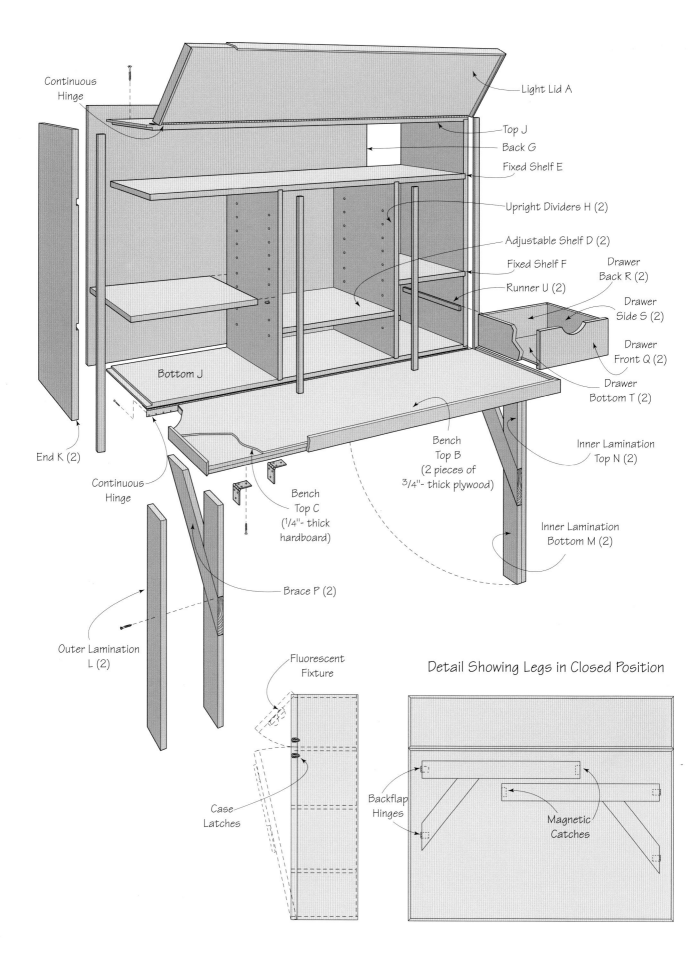

Continuous Hinge

Light Lid A

Top J

Back G

Fixed Shelf E

Upright Dividers H (2)

Adjustable Shelf D (2)

Fixed Shelf F

Runner U (2)

Drawer Back R (2)

Drawer Side S (2)

Drawer Front Q (2)

Drawer Bottom T (2)

Bottom J

End K (2)

Continuous Hinge

Outer Lamination L (2)

Brace P (2)

Bench Top C (1/4"- thick hardboard)

Bench Top B (2 pieces of 3/4"- thick plywood)

Inner Lamination Top N (2)

Inner Lamination Bottom M (2)

Fluorescent Fixture

Case Latches

Detail Showing Legs in Closed Position

Backflap Hinges

Magnetic Catches

inches (millimeters)

REFERENCE	QUANTITY	PART	STOCK	THICKNESS	(mm)	WIDTH	(mm)	LENGTH	(mm)	COMMENTS
A	1	light lid	plywood	3/4	(19)	11	(279)	57	(1448)	
B	2	bench tops	plywood	3/4	(19)	21 5/8	(549)	57	(1448)	2 pieces of 3/4 - thick plywood are laminated together to make top
C	1	bench top	hardboard	1/4	(6)	21 5/8	(549)	57	(1448)	
D	2	adjustable shelves	plywood	3/4	(19)	13 1/2	(343)	20 3/8	(518)	
E	1	long fixed shelf	plywood	3/4	(19)	13 1/2	(343)	57 1/2	(1461)	
F	1	short fixed shelf	plywood	3/4	(19)	13 1/2	(343)	14 5/8	(372)	
G	1	back	hardboard	1/4	(6)	35 1/2	(902)	58	(1473)	
H	2	upright dividers	plywood	3/4	(19)	13 1/2	(343)	22 1/2	(572)	
J	2	top and bottom	plywood	3/4	(19)	13 3/4	(349)	58	(1473)	
K	2	ends	plywood	3/4	(19)	13 3/4	(349)	36	(914)	
Leg assembly										
L	2	outer laminations	pine	3/4	(19)	3 1/2	(89)	34	(864)	
M	2	inner lamination bottoms	pine	3/4	(19)	3 1/2	(89)	22 1/2	(572)	45° angle one end
N	2	inner lamination tops	pine	3/4	(19)	3 1/2	(89)	10 1/2	(267)	45° angle one end
P	2	braces	pine	3/4	(19)	3 1/2	(89)	22	(559)	45° angle both ends
Drawers										
Q	2	fronts	birch plywood	1/2	(13)	5 1/2	(140)	14	(356)	
R	2	backs	birch plywood	1/2	(13)	5	(127)	13	(330)	
S	4	sides	birch plywood	1/2	(13)	5	(127)	12 3/4	(324)	
T	2	bottoms	hardboard	1/4	(6)	13 1/2	(343)	13	(330)	
U	2	runners	pine	1/2	(13)	3/4	(19)	12 3/4	(324)	

You will also need approximately 35' (11m) of 3/4" × 1/2" (19mm × 13mm) pine edging for the carcass and about 28' (9m) of 1 3/4" × 3/4" (45mm × 19mm) softwood edging for the bench top and light lid.

HARDWARE

Wood glue
3 36" (914mm) Piano hinges
4 1 1/2" (38mm) Back-flap hinges
2 Magnetic catches
3 Case latches
1 4' (122cm) Fluorescent light
4 Stays (for the light box)
   1 1/2" (38mm) No. 8 screws
   1 1/4" (32mm) No. 8 screws (to screw the legs together)
   5/16" × 1" (8mm × 25mm) Dowels
   Finishing nails

step 1

Cut the plywood to the correct sizes. Because the sheets are large and heavy, it is often easier to cut them with a circular saw rather than try to push them across the saw bench.

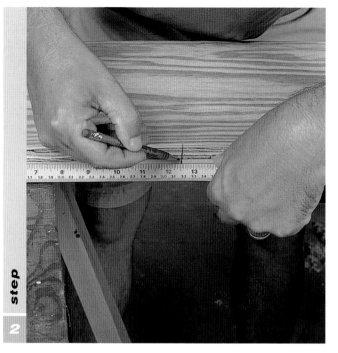

step 2

With the ends temporarily clamped face-to-face, measure down 12¹/₂" from one end and scribe a mark with a pencil. This is the top of the main shelf that divides the light box from the lower section.

step 3

Separate the two ends and square the lines across the inside faces. I am using a roofing square here, but any large square is fine. Avoid using a tool that will not reach across the board.

step 4

From this mark, square a parallel line exactly the width of the plywood shelf. An offcut is ideal for this. Make sure that the line is below the 12¹/₂" mark on each board, as it is easy to make a mistake. Then clamp a guide rail across the end for the router to run against. The template shown is made by measuring the distance from the edge of the straight router cutter to the edge of the base plate. This makes repetitive setting of the guide rail a snap.

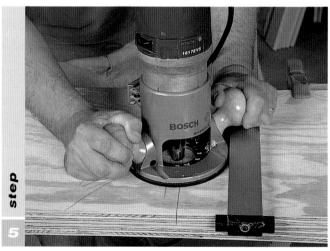

step 5

Rout a dado ¹/₄" deep across the end, keeping the base of the router tight to the rail. If you do not have a fancy rail like the one in the picture, a straight piece of wood clamped to the plywood works just as well. If your cutter is not the same width as the shelf is thick, you may need to move the guide and make a second pass.

With all the dadoes cut, rabbet for the hardboard back and the top and bottom. A bearing-guided cutter is perfect for this. Make the rabbet for the back $1/2$" deep by $1/4$" wide, as viewed from the face of the plywood panels. The rabbets for the plywood top and bottom panels are the same depths, but change the bearing to make the rabbet $3/4$" wide to suit the plywood.

Edge-band all the components with pine. Apply some glue and then use finishing nails to hold them in place. Set the heads below the surface with a nail set.

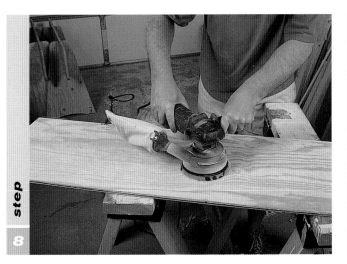

Sand all the parts, paying special attention to those that will be on the inside, as it is much easier now than when the job is assembled. Construction plywood is quite rough, so start with 80 grit and finish with 120 for a smooth surface.

Cut back the shelf edgings $1/4$" from the ends to allow for the difference between the depth of the dadoes and length of the shelves. You will need to cut the top and bottom back $1/2$" because the rabbets are deeper than the dadoes.

step 10

step 11

Glue and screw the top and bottom to the end panels. Use 1¹/₂" No. 8 screws, countersinking the heads just below the surface. Three screws are sufficient. Place one 2" in from the front and back edges and one on the center.

Glue and slide the long fixed shelf in from the back. You can see here why we had to cut the edging back. Wipe off any glue that runs down with a damp cloth. With the long shelf in place, glue in the two dividers and the short fixed shelf.

step 12

step 13

Cut the hardboard back and glue and pin this into the rabbet on the back of the cabinet. This will help hold the cabinet square while the glue sets.

This photo shows the completed main carcass. Remove sharp edges from the edgings and outside corners with a piece of 120-grit sandpaper.

14

Mark the insides of the drawer components and cut a groove ¹/₂" up from the bottom to accept the hardboard bottom. I cut mine with a slot cutter in the shaper, but a router will do the job just as well.

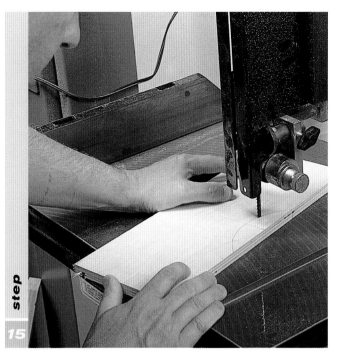

15

Draw and cut a radius on the drawer fronts to form the pulls. Use a fine-tooth blade in the band saw to minimize tear-out.

16

Smooth up the saw cuts with a foam sanding drum in the electric drill. An alternate method would be to wrap a piece of sandpaper around a section of dowel and rub out the scratches by hand.

17

Assemble the drawers with glue and finishing nails, nailing through the front and back into the ends. The bottom drawer simply rests on the cabinet base, but the upper drawer sits on runners pinned and glued in place as shown.

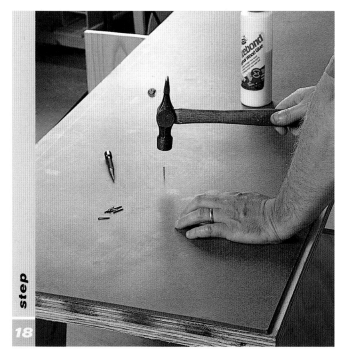

Make the bench top from two layers of plywood and a layer of hardboard. Using 1¼" screws, glue and screw the plywood together, then cover it with the hardboard to conceal the screws. A few 3d finishing nails through the hardboard will hold it in place as the glue sets.

Aligning two sheets of plywood and the hardboard accurately can be difficult, so I often find it easier to make the plywood a little oversize, then use a flush-trim bit in the router to bring the plywood down to the correct dimensions.

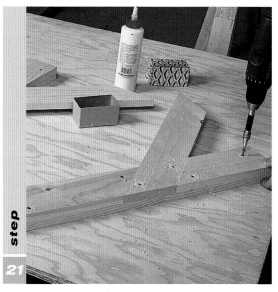

Lip the edges of the bench top and light lid, mitering it at the corners. When the glue is completely dry, fix the bench top and light lid to the carcass with a piano hinge. Most piano hinges come in 36" lengths, so you may have to cut a section of hinge to make a continuous length.

Make the leg assemblies, noting that there are right and left legs. Glue and screw the inner laminations to the outer section of each leg.

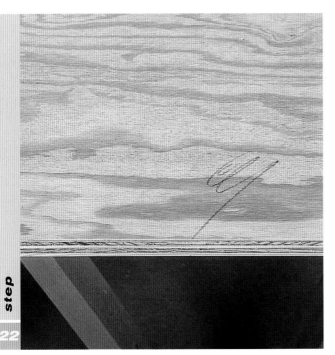

step 22

Mark the good side of the plywood and the front edges. This will help remind you how all the plywood parts fit together at assembly time.

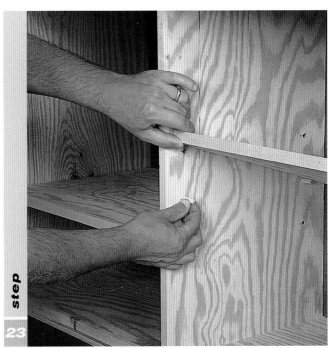

step 23

Wooden dowels make inexpensive and strong shelf pins. Set these about $1^1/_2$" from the front and back. Measure up 12" from the base, then space additional hole $2^1/_2$" up from there.

step 24

With the bench folded up, attach the back-flap hinges with No. 8 screws. If you refer to the drawing and final photo, you will note that these are staggered so that one leg clears the other.

TIP

Note that parts of the main carcass are handed; that is, the carcass has distinct left-hand and right-hand parts. To avoid mistakes, use marks to orient the parts. Keeping the marks on the inside of the job means that you are much less likely to cut the dadoes and rabbets incorrectly and end up with two parts that are the same. It is good practice to use these marks no matter how small or simple the job, as it will help you avoid frustration and save material from careless mistakes.

grinding BENCH

In my last workshop, I had my grinder mounted on a section of old kitchen worktop that was attached to a spare bit of wall with a couple of brackets. The trouble was that my workshop was a touch on the small side, and the grinding station always seemed to be in the way of my latest creation. Another problem that came to light only after I had used the grinder a few times was that the grime and grease seemed to find its way onto every clean timber surface in the shop, which did neither my temper nor the job any good at all. That cheap and cheerful bench stayed in the workshop after I moved out, and wanting somewhere new for my grinder, I knew that I could do better than that old worktop.

The answer is the bench you see here. Made simply from medium-density fiberboard (MDF), it is quick to build but heavy enough that it will not topple over. You could make it smaller if you wish, but the narrower it is, the less stable, so the dimensions I have used result in a bench that is not too big and that will not take up the whole workshop. In addition, the locking casters enable the bench to be pushed to where it is needed — alongside the lathe, for instance, when there is a need for frequent use — or pushed out of the way into an odd corner when it is not.

The shelf is an integral part of the construction, and apart from being a convenient spot for workshop supplies and tools, it takes the place of rails and keeps the bottom of the cabinet aligned.

Few tools and materials are needed to make this bench, and most of the components might well come from offcuts of a larger job. The most expensive parts are likely to be the casters, and although you could omit these, the versatility of the movable bench would be lost.

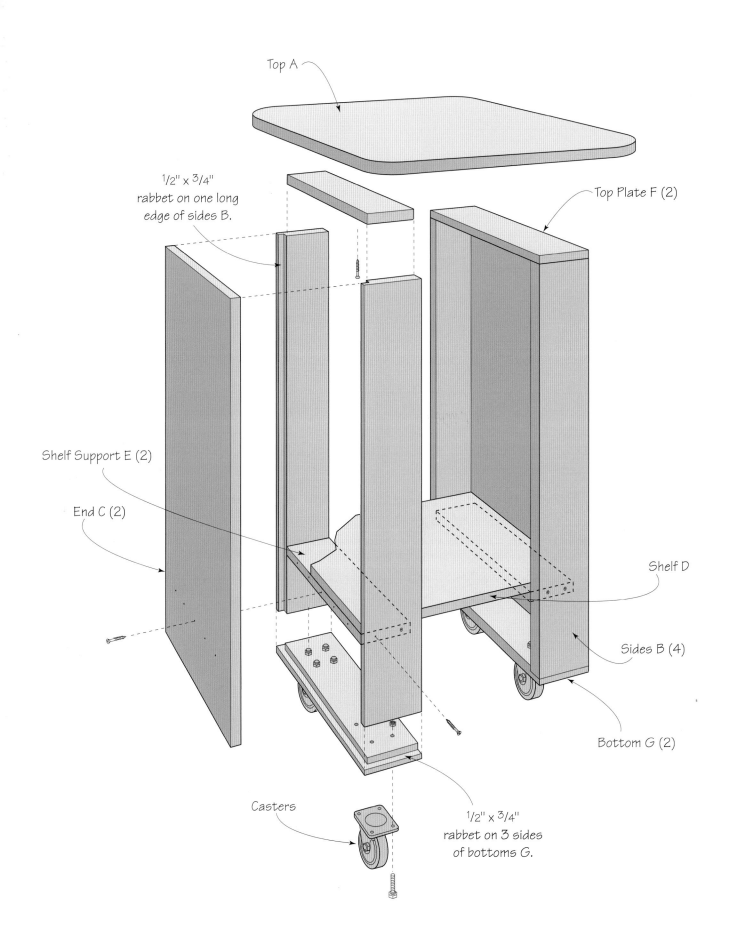

Top A

1/2" x 3/4" rabbet on one long edge of sides B.

Top Plate F (2)

Shelf Support E (2)

End C (2)

Shelf D

Sides B (4)

Bottom G (2)

Casters

1/2" x 3/4" rabbet on 3 sides of bottoms G.

inches (millimeters)

REFERENCE	QUANTITY	PART	STOCK	THICKNESS	(mm)	WIDTH	(mm)	LENGTH	(mm)	COMMENTS
A	1	top	MDF	3/4	(19)	21	(533)	24	(610)	
B	4	sides	MDF	3/4	(19)	5	(127)	33 1/2	(851)	
C	2	ends	MDF	3/4	(19)	17 3/4	(451)	33 1/2	(851)	
D	1	shelf	MDF	3/4	(19)	16 3/4	(425)	19 7/8	(505)	
E	2	shelf supports	MDF	3/4	(19)	4 1/4	(108)	16 3/4	(425)	
F	2	top plates	MDF	3/4	(19)	4 1/4	(108)	16 3/4	(425)	
G	2	bottoms	MDF	3/4	(19)	5	(127)	18 1/4	(464)	

HARDWARE

Wood glue
1 1/2" (38mm) No. 8 drywall screws
4 3" (76mm) Locking casters
16 Nuts, bolts and washers to suit casters
16 1/4"-20 × 1 1/4" (6mm-20 × 32mm) Hex-head bolts
16 1/4" (6mm) Washers
16 1/4"-20 (6mm-20) Nuts

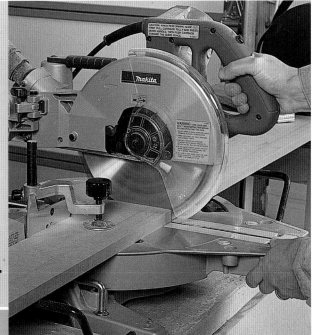

step 1

The first step in any job is cutting the components as per the cutting list. Cut them as accurately as you can, as any discrepancies will result in a twist in the bench and bits that do not fit together well. I find it easiest to cut the large sections of MDF and other sheet material to width with a circular saw, and then rather than try to maneuver large sheets across the circular saw table, I cut the sections to length with the miter saw.

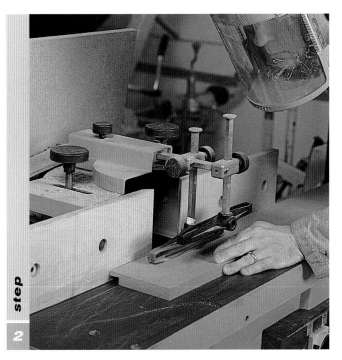

step 2

Rabbet the side pieces on the shaper or with a router. The rabbet should be 3/4" wide by 1/2" deep to accept the ends. Test the rabbet with a scrap to make sure that it is the right size. Note, too, that the side pieces are right- and left-handed as they are rabbeted down one long edge and across the bottom on one end only. Make sure that you end up with two of each hand. I like to mark in pencil where the rabbets are to go, so that I can be sure to make no mistakes.

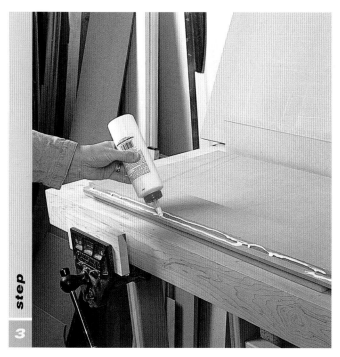

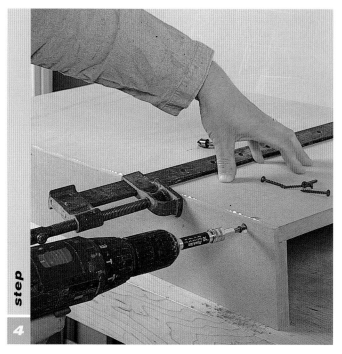

step 3

Lay the end pieces flat on the bench, then apply a generous bead of glue to the rabbet that you have formed on the side pieces. MDF is quite porous where it has been machined and will soak up quite a lot of glue. Experience will tell you how much to apply; not too much that it squeezes out everywhere, but not too little that the joint is starved of glue.

step 4

Use a clamp to hold the side pieces snug to the end as you screw them together. Three or four screws per side is ample, but do make sure that you do not put the screws closer than $1^{1}/_{2}$" to the end or there is a chance of splitting the MDF.

step 5

This close-up of fitting the bottoms shows how the screws should be placed. The surface of the MDF is quite hard, and for a neat job you have to countersink the screw heads. Unlike many types of timber, MDF has no give and the heads will not pull below the surface.

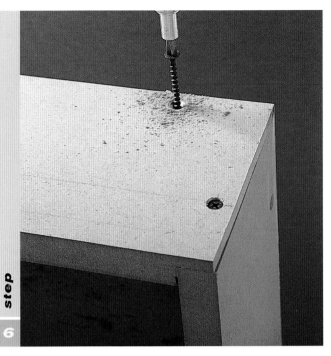

Drill a pilot hole and drive the screw as shown here. I use dry-wall screws, which are cheap and will hold the MDF together far better than standard wood screws. A little paraffin on the threads will help the screws to go in a little bit easier.

Glue and screw the top plates in place between the side pieces, keeping them flush with the ends of the side and end pieces. This part will hold the top in place with screws from underneath.

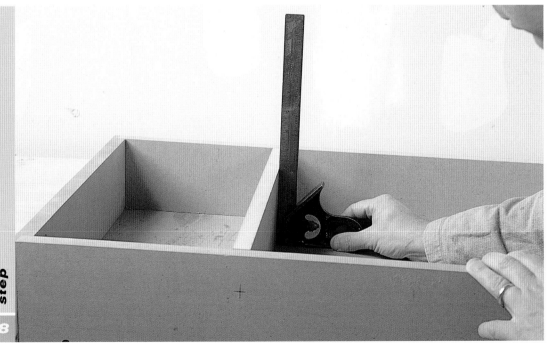

The shelf supports are exactly the same size as the top plates. Glue and screw these in position 7" up from the bottom. Be very careful about checking these parts for square and alignment as you fit them, as any discrepancy will prevent the shelf from fitting correctly and impart twist, which will make the bench wobble.

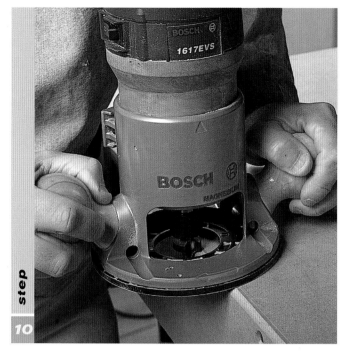

Stand the two ends right way up on some sawhorses on a bench and insert the shelf. I prefer not to glue this in place in case I ever have to take the bench apart later. Three screws on each side driven up through the shelf supports are more than adequate.

Run a bearing-guided roundover bit around the box edges to remove the sharp corners, but do not rout the top edge where the worktop is to be attached.

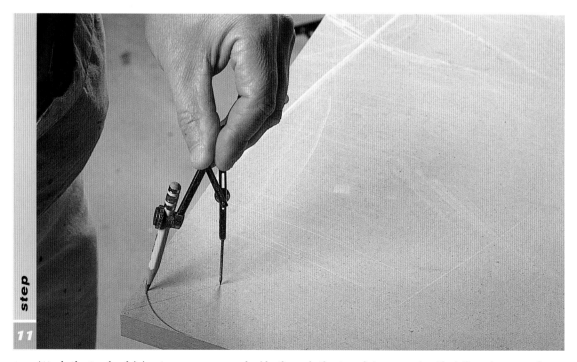

Attach the top by driving two screws up each side through the top plates, ensuring that there is an equal margin at each side and front and back. Then use a pair of compasses to mark a radius on each corner. If you can't find your compasses, then drawing around a paint can works just as well.

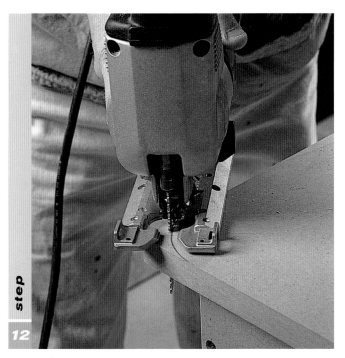

step 12

With a fine blade in the jigsaw, cut accurately to the line before smoothing with sandpaper wrapped around a block.

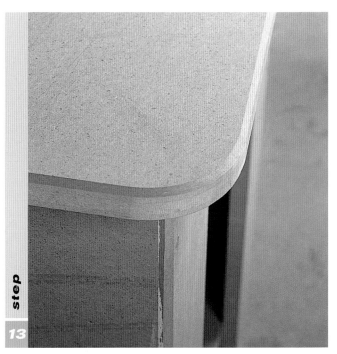

step 13

To finish the top, take off the sharp top edge. I used a 45° bevel bearing-guided cutter, but a roundover bit would work just as well.

step 14

The final job is to fit the casters. Turn the bench upside down and use nuts, bolts and washers suitable for the casters to attach them to the bottom. Note that I have used locking casters for the sake of safety, as they prevent the bench from rolling away or moving while it is being used.

WORKBENCH

This large table was made for my wife, who kept suggesting that although I had many benches in my workshop, she had nowhere to do her sewing. What she needed was a large flat table on which she could lay out her material, patterns and other sewing materials. Furthermore the table, or "bench," as she likes to call it, needed a smooth top that would not catch delicate material, fibers and threads.

Another design criteria was that the bench should not look out of place in our New England colonial home, but blend in with the décor and surroundings; in short, it should look like a piece of furniture.

After some head scratching, I think that I have succeeded. All the materials came from my local home store and cost less than $175, excluding the paint, which I already had. Once I had worked out how I was going to go about the project, I completed the bench in less than a day. The turned legs look classy, but these are simply stair newel posts with the ends trimmed. The top is made, like some of the other projects in this book, from a door, which gives a perfectly flat and smooth work surface, my wife's main requirement. I could have made the bench with square legs, but I don't think that it would have blended so well with the house.

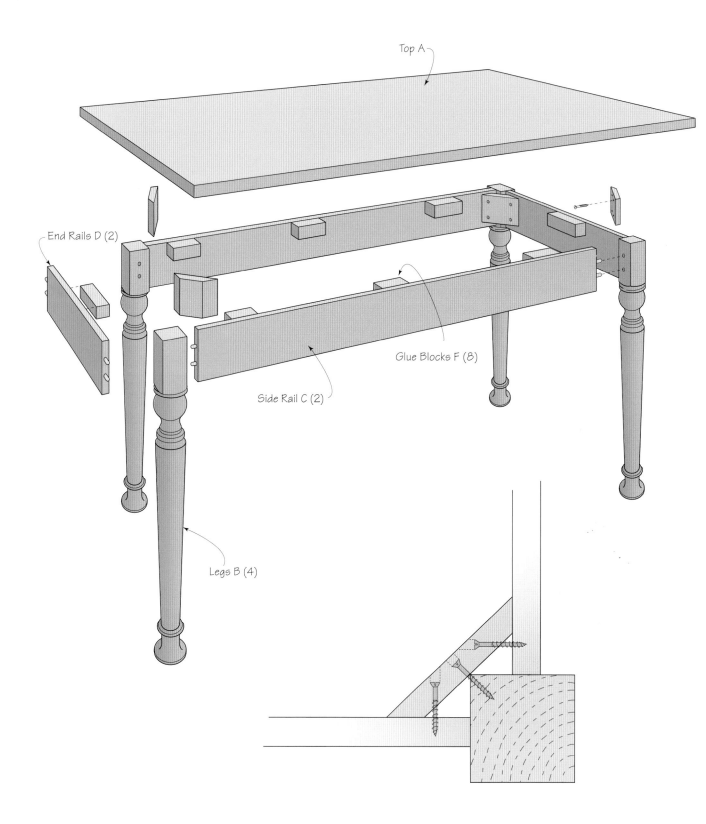

Top A

End Rails D (2)

Side Rail C (2)

Glue Blocks F (8)

Legs B (4)

inches (millimeters)

REFERENCE	QUANTITY	PART	STOCK	THICKNESS	(mm)	WIDTH	(mm)	LENGTH	(mm)	COMMENTS
A	1	top	door	1½	(38)	36	(914)	81	(2057)	hollow-core door blank
B	4	legs	pine	3	(76)	3	(76)	29	(737)	cut from newel post
C	2	side rails	pine	¾	(19)	5½	(140)	65	(1651)	
D	2	end rails	pine	¾	(19)	5½	(140)	21	(533)	
E	4	corner braces	pine	¾	(19)	4	(102)	6	(152)	mark exact length from frame
F	8	glue blocks	pine	1½	(38)	1½	(38)	3	(76)	

You will also need approximately 19½" (496mm) of ⅛" × 1½" (3mm × 38mm) wood edging that matches the door blank.

HARDWARE

Wood glue
5/16" (8mm) Dowels
1¼" (32mm) No. 10 screws
Masking tape

step 1

Cut the newel posts to length to form the legs. First, cut off the top square section of the newel post, where the handrail normally attaches. Cut just above the pommel, leaving this intact as it forms the foot. Measure up from the cut 29" and mark the leg at this point. Cut the leg at this mark. This should leave you at least 5½" of square section to attach the rails to later.

Clean up the end and rails so that they are $^3/_8$" narrower than the height of the square section at the top of the leg. I did not have much to take off, so I could do this with a No. 8 plane. If you have much to take off, rip it down on the table saw before you plane the edge smooth.

Mark for the dowels, which should be positioned in thirds. A handy trick to easily mark out the centers and to divide the rail into thirds without complicated math is to slant a ruler across the face of the board until the measurement reads a number easily divisible by 3; in this case, 6. Then mark the face at 2" and 4", draw these parallel to the edge and across the ends and, voilà, perfect spacing.

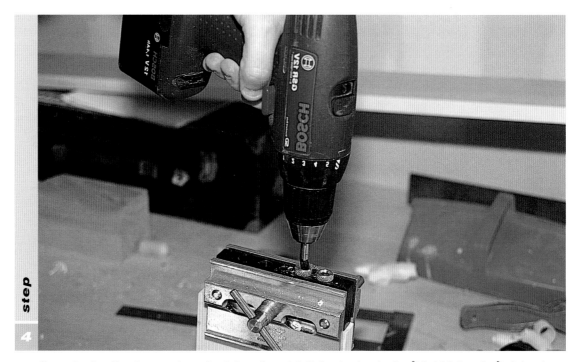

Clamp the doweling jig onto the ends of the rails and drill for the dowels. For $^3/_4$"-thick boards, $^5/_{16}$" dowels offer a good strong joint without weakening the board.

Gauge a line 1³/₈" from the outside face of the leg. Transfer the center lines for the dowels and drill a ⁵/₁₆" hole. Apply glue to the joint and dowels and assemble the parts.

Use a band clamp to hold the bench together and then check for square. Fit corner braces made from 4"-wide timbers across the corners to reinforce the joint. These are glued and screwed in position ³/₄" down from the top edge of the rail. The inside faces should just kiss the inner corner of the leg.

You can see here how the corner brace is fitted. Note that the inside face just clears the corner of the leg. Although this is sufficient to hold the corner square, I like to drive a screw through the center of the brace, into the corner of the leg for extra rigidity.

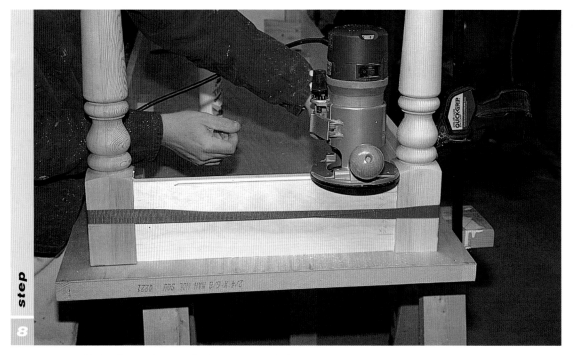

Rout a small detail moulding on the bottom edge of the rails with a bearing-guided cutter in the router. You can do this before assembly, but as you can see, the legs act as a stop, ensuring that the bead stops an equal distance from each corner.

Here is a view of the completed moulding, which I feel looks more professional than a moulding running right into the corners. Do not make the moulding too large, but by all means use a different cutter to suit your tastes. This is definitely one of those times when less is more.

With the frame still upside down, attach the top with glue blocks. Use three on each side rail, equally spaced, and one at each end. If making this bench with a solid top, use stretcher plates or buttons, which allow for the movement of the top. As it is, the door blank will not move and it is safe to glue in place.

Cut some $1/8$"-thick strips made from wood similar to the face veneer on the door, and glue these to the ends of the top to disguise the door. Because these are so thin and light, masking tape is more than enough to hold the strips as the glue sets. When dry, remove the tape and cut the strips flush with the top and ends.

low bench

TOOL TOTE

This little bench has to be one of the most useful pieces in my workshop. Wider than a standard sawhorse, the top provides a stable platform for sawing and working on bits of wood near the job. Its height makes it comfortable for holding wood with my foot or knee, and it is sturdy enough to take my full weight if I need to reach up high.

An added bonus of this bench is the tool tray, which is large enough to hold a fair amount of tools, certainly enough for most on-site jobs. The hand hole in the top makes transporting the bench easy, if a little heavy when full of tools. The tools add a little to the stability of the bench.

Quick and inexpensive to make, it requires little in the way of skill, but as with all the projects in this book, care taken in the construction will pay dividends in the longevity of the bench. I made mine from select pine boards, but it could be made from plywood, although it is not quite so forgiving to tools and hands. But use what you have, by all means. Make a rough version to start, but I guarantee that you will find the bench so handy that you might well end up making a couple of them.

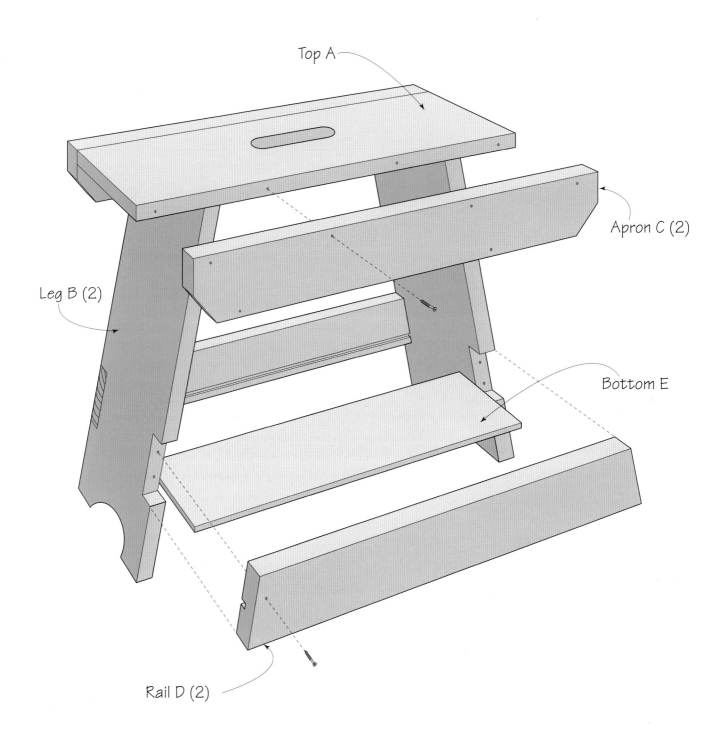

Top A

Apron C (2)

Leg B (2)

Bottom E

Rail D (2)

inches (millimeters)

REFERENCE	QUANTITY	PART	STOCK	THICKNESS	(mm)	WIDTH	(mm)	LENGTH	(mm)	COMMENTS
A	1	top	pine	7/8	(22)	9	(229)	30	(762)	
B	2	legs	pine	7/8	(22)	9	(229)	20	(508)	bevel both ends
C	2	aprons	pine	7/8	(22)	3½	(89)	30	(762)	
D	2	rails	pine	7/8	(22)	3½	(89)	28	(711)	
E	1	bottom	hardboard	¼	(6)	8¼	(209)	25½	(648)	

HARDWARE

Wood glue
1½" (38mm) No. 8 screws

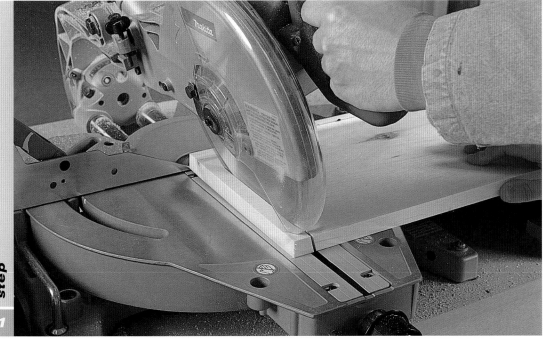

step 1

The first thing to do is to cut all the components to length. The top is cut straight across at both ends.
Note that the legs have a 15° angle cut on both top and bottom.

Set your sliding bevel to the same angle that you cut on the bottom and top of the legs. Use this to mark the shoulders for the rail housings. Put the first line 4" up from the bottom of the leg. Then use a section of timber of similar dimensions to the rail, and with this against the first shoulder line, draw another line across the leg, thus marking the width of the housing. Square the marks across the face and mark the other edge of the leg. Mark the second leg in identical fashion.

Use a marking gauge and, between the pencil lines that you drew across the face of the legs, gauge a line the exact thickness of the rail.

Clamp the two legs together in the vise with the bevel marks exactly aligned with each other and the edges flush. Use a fine saw to cut down the pencil lines to the gauge marks.

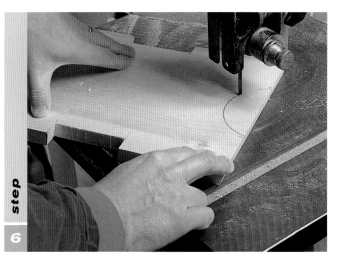

step 5

Now it becomes evident why I clamped the two legs together; this provides more support for the base of the router. With a straight cutter in the router, remove the waste between the saw cuts down to the gauge lines. If using a small-diameter cutter or a lightweight router, you may have to take the waste out in several passes until you reach the correct depth.

step 6

Using a narrow band saw blade, cut out the semicircular waste, thus forming the two feet. I measured in about $2^{1}/_{2}$" from each side and drew the line around a convenient paint can. With this cut out, clean up the inside of the radius with some 120-grit paper. The more accurate your cut, the less smoothing that you have to do.

step 7

With the legs complete, put these to one side and prepare the top. A generous oval-shaped hole in the top acts as both a handhold and convenient spot to place a clamp when working on bigger pieces of wood after the bench is completed. Drill two $1^{3}/_{4}$"-diameter holes about 5" apart on the center line of the top and cut between them with a jigsaw. If you do not have any large-diameter drill bits, drill a smaller hole and cut the whole thing out with a fine-tooth jigsaw blade.

Cut the grooves for the $^1/_4$" hardboard bottom in the rails. These are $^3/_4$" from the bottom edge of the rails and $^1/_2$" deep. Use a scrap of hardboard to check for a snug fit. I cut the grooves using a slotting cutter in the shaper, but a router table will do the job just as quickly.

Glue and screw one of the rails into the housings in the legs, then turn the assembly over and slide the bottom into the groove. Note that no grooves are cut into the legs; the hardboard is simply cut to be a good fit between the legs. If you intend to place lots of heavy tools in the tray, nail some $^3/_4$" × $^3/_4$" battens to support the hardboard and prevent it from sagging.

Now you can glue and screw the second rail in position, but do a dry run first to check the fit. Especially check the hardboard, as if this is a little wide, it will prevent the rail from sitting into the housings. If this happens, remove the hardboard bottom, take a few passes with a sharp plane and recheck. When you are happy with the fit, spread on a little adhesive and drive the screws home. I predrilled and countersunk the holes to both avoid splitting the wood and give a neat appearance.

The aprons are fitted next. These are glued and screwed flush with the top surface, and in line with the ends. Drive screws into the legs as shown to secure the top to the completed leg assembly.

Place the bench on a level surface. If it wobbles at all, use a sharp plane to trim a little off the high foot. Finally, use a sandpaper block and 120-grit abrasive to remove all the sharp edges. The bench is now complete and ready for work, although for a deluxe finish you could give it a couple of coats of polyurethane varnish.

metalworking

BENCH

As a woodworker, I do from time to time have the need for a spot of metalworking. I prefer to work in wood rather than metal, but on the occasion that I do have to cut any sections of metal, I like to keep them well away from my wood. Therefore, this bench is a woodworker's metalworking bench; heavy enough for the odd bit of metalwork but small enough that it will not take over the whole of the workshop or garage.

It is quick to make, too. The metal legs simply bolt together, and the top is a section of kitchen countertop. The laminated top is easy to clean, and the vise holds even the heaviest sections of metal. The hardest part of all is probably the drawer, which I have added to store one or two metalworking tools, such as files, wrenches and hacksaws. Although you could remove the drawer, I do think that it is a good idea as it keeps tools that may be contaminated with grease and dirt away from your precious woodworking tools.

The bottom shelf can be used for anything from engine parts to power tools and provides rigidity to the bench. I added the upright backboard to prevent oil splashes and spills from marking the walls, but it has the added benefit of allowing tool racks and workshop fixtures to be easily attached.

One word of caution, however; when bolting the frame together, check everything for square before finally tightening up the bolts with a wrench.

I bought a predrilled steel angle bar from my local home center, but a cold-rolled steel angle bar works just as well, though you will have to spend a little time drilling for the bolts.

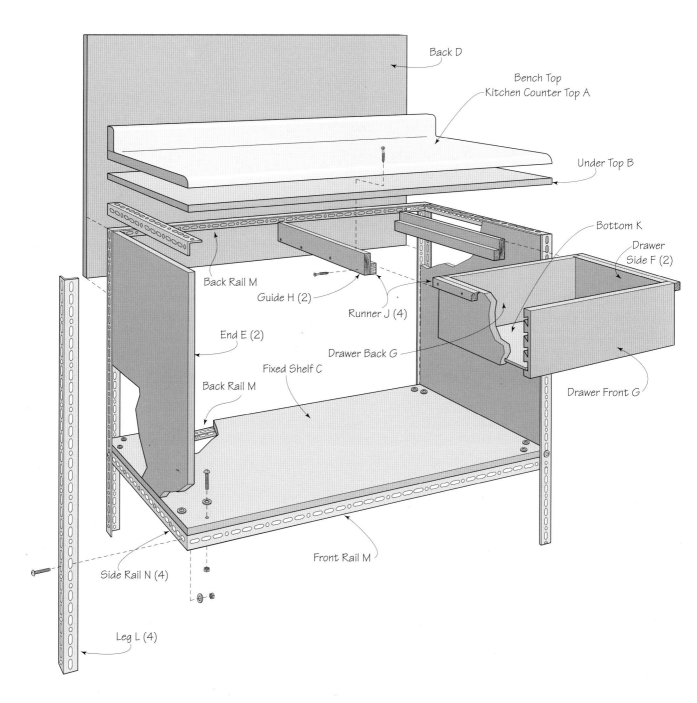

Back D

Bench Top
Kitchen Counter Top A

Under Top B

Bottom K

Drawer
Side F (2)

Back Rail M

Guide H (2)

Runner J (4)

Drawer Back G

End E (2)

Fixed Shelf C

Drawer Front G

Back Rail M

Side Rail N (4)

Front Rail M

Leg L (4)

inches (millimeters)

REFERENCE	QUANTITY	PART	STOCK	THICKNESS	(mm)	WIDTH	(mm)	LENGTH	(mm)	COMMENTS
A	1	bench top	particleboard	1	(25)	25½	(648)	49	(1245)	section of premade countertop
B	1	under top	MDF	¾	(19)	24½	(623)	49	(1245)	
C	1	fixed shelf	MDF	¾	(19)	24½	(623)	48	(1219)	
D	1	back	MDF	¾	(19)	30	(762)	49	(1245)	
E	2	ends	particleboard	¾	(19)	24	(610)	24	(610)	
F	2	drawer sides	pine	¾	(19)	5½	(140)	21½	(546)	
G	2	drawer front & back	pine	¾	(19)	5½	(140)	18	(457)	
H	2	drawer guides	pine	¾	(19)	2½	(64)	21½	(546)	
J	4	drawer runners	pine	¾	(19)	1	(25)	21½	(546)	
K	1	drawer bottom	hardboard	¼	(6)	21¼	(539)	16⅞	(428)	

Metalwork (cut from predrilled, galvanized steel 1½" × 1½" [38mm × 38mm] angle bar)

REFERENCE	QUANTITY	PART	STOCK	THICKNESS	(mm)	WIDTH	(mm)	LENGTH	(mm)	COMMENTS
L	4	legs						36	(914)	
M	3	(1) front and (2) back rails						48	(1219)	
N	4	side rails						24	(610)	

HARDWARE

1½" (38mm) No. 8 screws
Metalwork vise
¼" (6mm) Bolts, nuts and washers ½" (13mm) and 1¼" (32mm) long

step 1

Cut the metal legs and other components to size. The reason I made the bench this size is that all the metal components came from my home store in either 4' or 6' lengths. To avoid damaging your woodworking bench, clamp the steel angle bar to a sawhorse.

step 2

File the ends to remove all sharp edges. If your sawing has been less than perfect, this is the time to square the cuts with the file. Although it might look like I am using a wood rasp in the picture, this is actually a double-sided file with a half-cut metal tooth on one side and a wood rasp on the other.

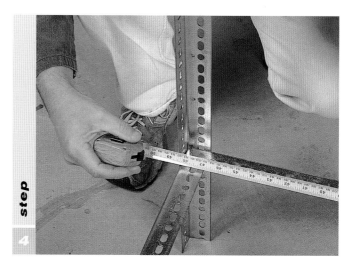

Once you have all the metal cut, bolt everything together. Note that where the legs meet the rails, the bolts are on the inside faces of the legs. Check for square before tightening the bolts with a wrench.

Take accurate measurements directly from the frame to determine the exact size of the fixed shelf, which should be a snug fit between the upright legs.

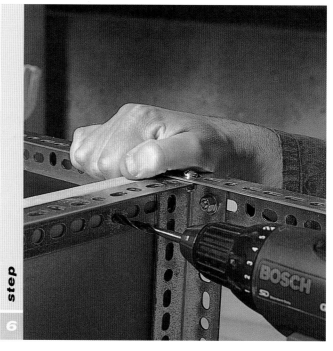

Use a bearing-guided bevel cutter in a router to remove the sharp edges on both sides of the shelf when using MDF. It makes a neater appearance, removes any slight roughness in the edges and will prevent tools and equipment from catching the edge when they are slid onto the shelf after installation.

With the shelf in position, drill from the underside for the bolts. Use a 5/16" drill bit to give plenty of clearance for the 1/4" bolts.

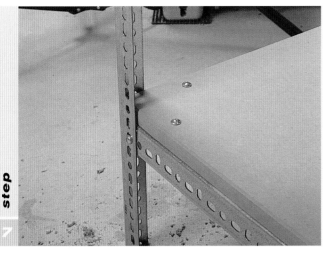

This photo shows the fixed shelf bolted into position. Use eight nuts and 1¹/₄" bolts in total. Each bolt should be positioned about 2" in from the corner, but the exact location is determined by the predrilled holes in the steel angle bar. With the fixed shelf in position, repeat the procedure for the under top. Note, however, from the cutting list that it is slightly larger than the fixed shelf to allow it to slightly overlap the legs and rails at the top. Next, refer to the drawing and fit the back panel with four nuts and bolts, keeping the bottom edge 25¹/₂" up from the bottom of the legs.

Make the drawer by dovetailing the sides into the front and back. If you do not have a jig, cut the joints by hand. Because the drawer will support a lot of weight, dovetails are the only suitable joint.

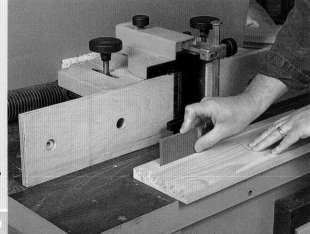

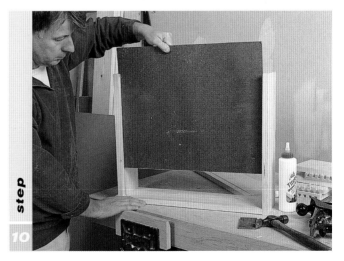

Cut a groove ³/₈" deep around the inside of the box for the drawer bottom, suitable for ¹/₄" hardboard or plywood. Use a router or a shaper for this. Do not put the groove too close to the bottom; make it at least ³/₄" up from the bottom edge. Check with a scrap of hardboard to make sure the groove is not too tight.

There is no need to glue the bottom in place, as the dovetails are more than adequate to hold the drawer together. Place the drawer down on a flat surface and allow to the glue to dry after checking for square.

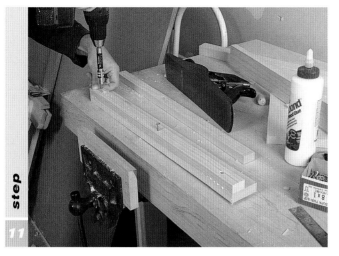

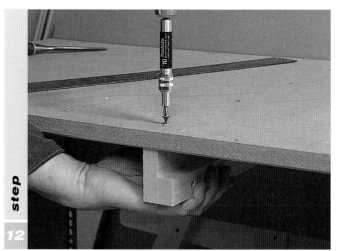

step 11

Make each of the two drawer runner assemblies by gluing and screwing one of the $3/4" \times 1"$ drawer runners flush with the bottom of one of the drawer guides. Glue and screw the other two drawer runners onto each side of the drawer, making these flush with the top surface.

step 12

Fit the drawer runner assemblies under the MDF under top. Fit one side first, ensuring that it is both flush with the front edge of the under top and square to the front edge. Then place the drawer in position and use the width of the drawer to determine the placement of the other drawer runner assembly. Drill, glue and screw this in place.

step 13

Fit the bench top by screwing up from below through the under top. You should need no more than six screws; three near the front edge and three near the back. You can also put a couple through the back panel, too, if your bench top has a backsplash. Then drill for the vise bolts; the exact position of these will depend on the vise used.

OVERSIZE PANELS

Many of the projects in this book require you to be able to cut panels to size accurately. Working alone and handling large, heavy sheets over the table saw can be difficult and dangerous. I prefer to cut the panels with a circular saw, resting the panel on a couple of sawhorses. After marking the panel, I clamp a guide for the base of the saw to run against. I have had good results with these aluminum guides that have an integral clamp, but a straightedge and a couple of C-clamps work just as well; it just takes a little more time to set up. Because the blade is offset somewhat from the side of the base plate, I have made a plywood template equal to this distance that I use to offset the guide to the right of the line, thus ensuring that the saw blade cuts exactly to my marks.

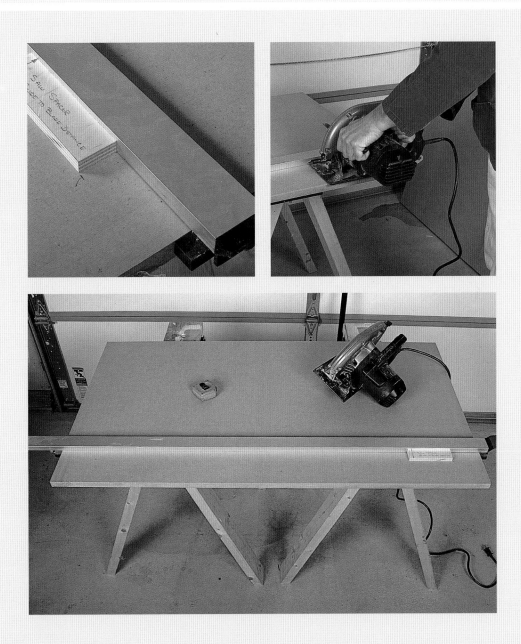

miter SAW BENCH

One of the most used tools in my workshop is my miter saw. Fast and accurate, it has cut its way through countless lengths of lumber, moulding and trim. Excellent as they may be, miter saws all suffer from one serious drawback: the lack of support on either side of the cut for longer lengths of lumber. Not only does this make less accurate cuts, but the chance of getting lumber kicked back toward you is increased. As I use my saw exclusively in the workshop for cutting material to length, nothing prevents the saw from being bolted down to some sort of extension table.

The simplest method when making any bench to hold a saw of this sort would be to affix it to the wall in the workshop. The main advantage of attaching a bench to the wall is that the whole structure can be very rigid and strong, but the downside of this is that it is permanently fixed in one spot. As my workshop is constantly evolving, I wanted to be able to move the bench from time to time to suit my work needs and changing workshop.

To be effective and accurate, the bench must be strong and resistant to flex and distortion, as a bench that is not accurately made will transfer any error to the work being cut. Sheet material is ideal for this project, as it is both strong and resistant to movement. I used ¾" medium-density fiberboard (MDF), which has a smooth surface and is dimensionally stable. An alternative would be plywood, although unless you use the best quality, this might have a less-than-perfect surface.

As with all the projects in this book, nothing in this one should trouble the competent woodworker, but I cannot overemphasize the need for care and accuracy in the marking and cutting of the parts. This is especially true of the fence components. Take your time and make sure everything is square, and the bench will repay you handsomely in your future woodworking projects.

Sheet material comes in 8' lengths, so this is the overall length of the bench. You could make it longer if you wish, but this would mean joining sheets end to end, which introduces another chance for inaccuracies to creep into the construction. In any event, 8' is more than adequate for most projects, with 4' on each side of the blade.

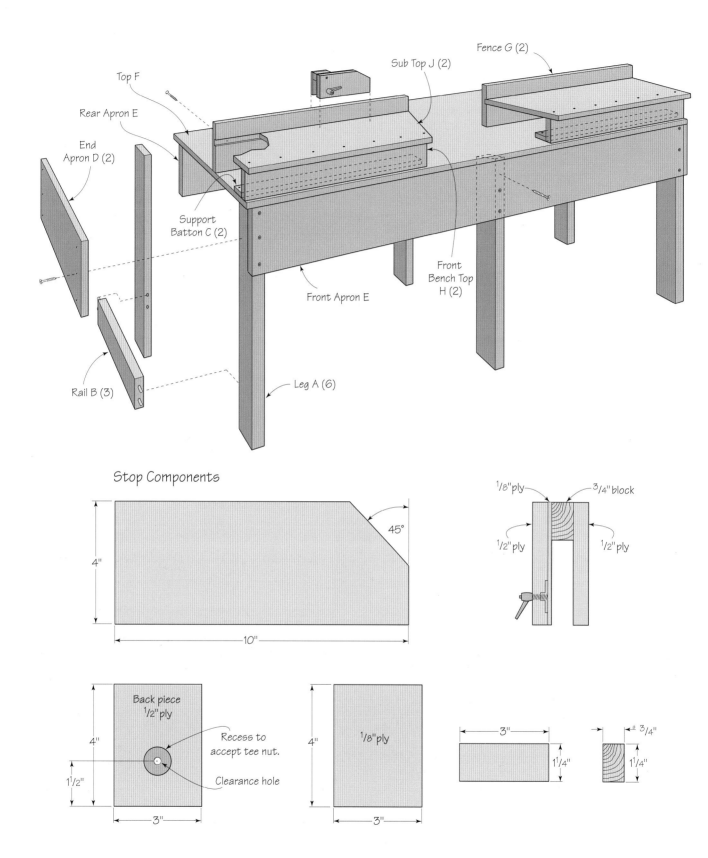

Fence G (2)

Sub Top J (2)

Top F

Rear Apron E

End
Apron D (2)

Support
Batton C (2)

Front
Bench Top
H (2)

Front Apron E

Rail B (3)

Leg A (6)

Stop Components

45°

4"

10"

1/8"ply
3/4" block

1/2" ply
1/2" ply

Back piece
1/2" ply

Recess to
accept tee nut.

Clearance hole

4"

1 1/2"

3"

1/8"ply

4"

3"

3"

1 1/4"

3/4"

1 1/4"

inches (millimeters)

REFERENCE	QUANTITY	PART	STOCK	THICKNESS	(mm)	WIDTH	(mm)	LENGTH	(mm)	COMMENTS
A	6	legs	pine	2	(51)	4	(102)	32	(813)	
B	3	rails	pine	2	(51)	4	(102)	21	(533)	
C	2	support battens	pine	1	(25)	2³/₄	(70)	33¹/₄	(844)	
D	2	end aprons	MDF	³/₄	(19)	9	(229)	29³/₄	(756)	
E	2	front & rear aprons	MDF	³/₄	(19)	9	(229)	95³/₄	(2432)	
F	1	top	MDF	³/₄	(19)	29³/₄	(756)	96³/₄	(2457)	
G	2	fences	MDF	³/₄	(19)	7	(178)	38	(965)	
H	2	front bench tops	MDF	³/₄	(19)	3³/₄	(95)	33¹/₄	(844)	width depends on height of saw
J	2	subtops	MDF	³/₄	(19)	11	(279)	38	(965)	
Stop										
K	1	back piece	plywood	¹/₂	(13)	3	(76)	4	(102)	
L	1	spacer	plywood	¹/₈	(3)	3	(76)	4	(102)	
M	1	inside face	pine	³/₄	(19)	1¹/₄	(32)	3	(76)	
N	1	face piece	plywood	¹/₂	(13)	4	(102)	10	(254)	

HARDWARE

Wood glue
1¹/₂" (38mm) No. 8 drywall screws
⁵/₁₆" (8mm) Dowels
Miter saw
Nuts, bolts and washers to mount saw
¹/₄"-20 (6mm-20) T-nut

step 1

After cutting all the material as specified in the cutting list, cut the rabbets on the end aprons. Rather than rely on the router's fence, I prefer to clamp a straightedge on top of the board and run the router against this, as there is less chance of the router wobbling at the beginning or end of the cut.

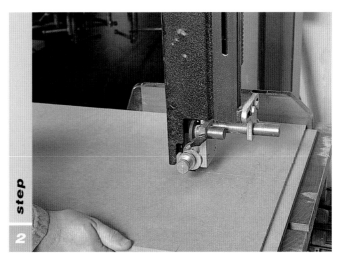

step 2

You may find it easier to cut the rabbets on a board wider than you will need, although of the correct length, and rip these down to the correct width after machining.

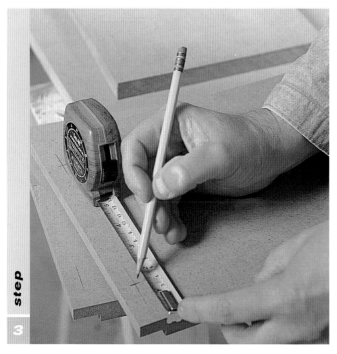

Mark for the screws that attach the end aprons to the front and rear aprons. Measure $1^{1}/_{2}$" in from each edge and $^{3}/_{8}$" in from the ends. This will ensure that when the screws are driven they will not come through the face of the boards.

Drill the pilot hole, spread on a bead of glue and screw the end aprons onto the front and rear aprons. Use a clamp to hold the parts together if you find it easier.

Screw down the top to the apron assembly and place the screws at 10" centers. Notice that the top is cut a little larger than the overall size of the apron assembly. This is trimmed off later and ensures a neat job. It is easy to get the apron assembly out of square at this stage, so set the apron assembly level and square on a couple of sawhorses and do not move it again until the top is fixed.

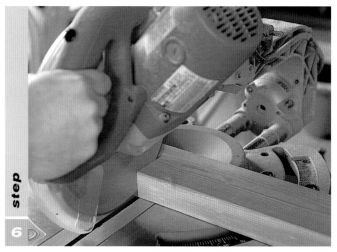

The top is supported on six legs, which must be cut exactly the same length. Cut them all slightly long, then cut them to exact length all at once. If you are taller than my 5'10", you could increase the length, which will in turn raise the bench height and reduce fatigue on your back.

Mark out the position of the rails on the inside of the legs. Put all the legs together on the bench and mark them all at once. Square a line across the lumber 8" up from the bottom. Place one of the rails against the top side of this line and scribe a line to mark the exact width of the rails.

Square a line across, 1" in from each of these two shoulder lines, and use this to position the doweling jig. Make corresponding marks onto the ends of the rails, also. This ensures that both joints go together without a hitch. Drill for $5/16$" dowels.

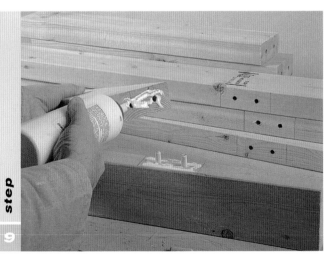

Glue the dowels into the legs, then set the rails down onto the dowels, ensuring that you use plenty of glue. Clamp and check for square before setting aside to allow the glue to set.

When the legs are completely dry, turn the bench top over and rest it on a couple of sawhorses. Set the legs into each end and screw through the aprons to fix in position. The intermediate leg sits exactly in the center of the bench. This is fixed by screwing through the front and rear aprons.

With the bench the right way up, trim off the excess bench top overhang with a flush-trim bearing-guided cutter in the router.

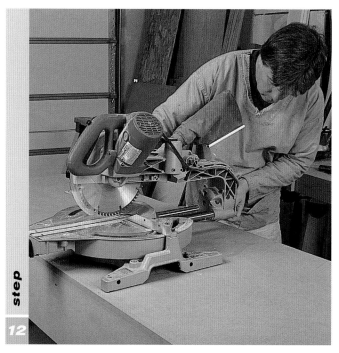

Set the saw temporarily in position on the bench top. Do not worry about exact placement at this stage. We just need to mark some of the components before they are machined.

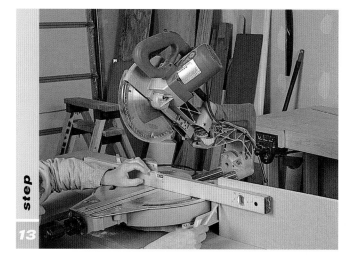

Stand one of the fences next to the saw and use a straight-edge to transfer the top surface height to the MDF. You need to do this with only one piece, as both fences are identical.

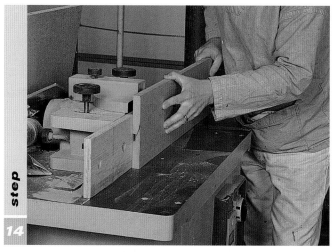

The line denotes the topmost mark of the housing for the subtop. Machine the housing $3/8$" deep to accept the MDF subtop.

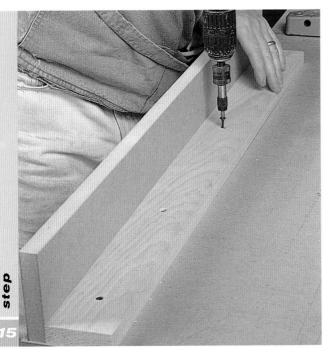

Screw down the softwood support battens, which support the front bench tops. Then screw the front bench tops to this, through the front into the batten. I do not glue this, as I may need to adjust this at some time and any adhesive would make adjustment impossible.

Next, screw the subtop to the fence through the back of the fence.

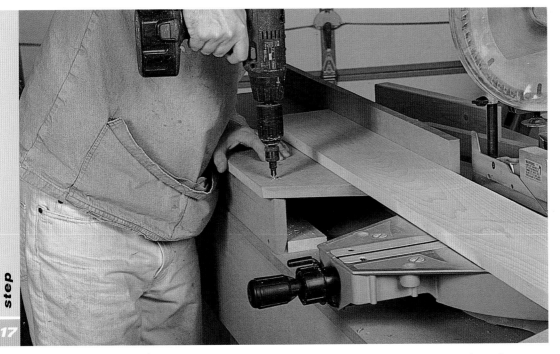

Use a long straightedge to align the two fence faces so that there are no gaps. Do not worry about the saw fence at this stage, just concentrate on getting the wooden fences aligned with each other. Check that you have a 3/4" overhang on the front before screwing in position. Check constantly as you do this to make sure that the fences do not move.

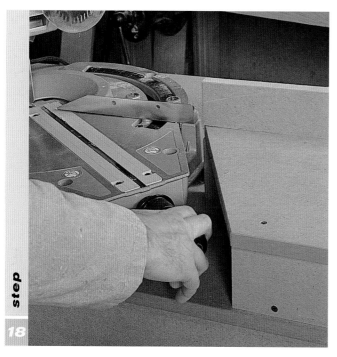

Check the action of the saw table with the saw in the correct position; do not bolt it down just yet. In this photo you can see the slope on the bench top that allows the table to rotate.

Use a square to make sure that the fence is upright and square to the subtop. A clamp can be put to good use to pull a slightly out-of-square fence. When you are happy with the position of the fence, screw from underneath to fix the fence in place.

Use a block plane to remove all the sharp edges.

Place the straightedge across the tabletop and move the saw back and forth until the saw fence is perfectly aligned with the wooden fences on either side. Then drill down through the saw mounting holes, through the table, and bolt the saw in place. Double-check that the saw has not moved before finally tightening the nuts.

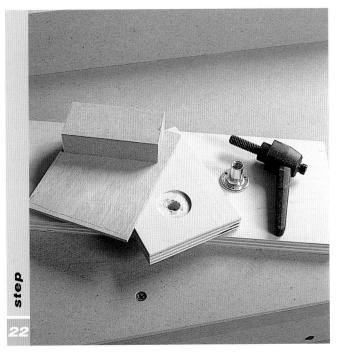

The stop is a simple construction that may be used on either side of the saw. This picture shows the components before assembly. Note the counterbore to accept the flange of the T-nut. Refer to the exploded drawing to see how all the parts fit together.

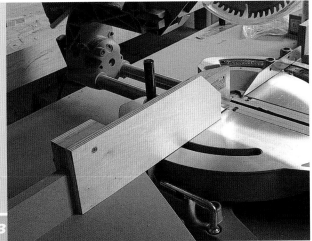

The stop is in position on the fence to the left of the saw blade. The long front section allows it to move right up to the blade. Some builders of crosscut saw benches set tape measures into the fence. I prefer not to do this as it can be set up accurately to only one particular blade, and at best is only a rough guide. I set the position of the stop by using a standard tape measure between the lowered stopped blade and fence, which is accurate no matter which blade is fitted into the saw.

This is a detail photo of the back of the stop. It shows the ratchet lever, which clamps it to the fence.

SAWHORSES

Although a workbench is at the heart of just about every woodworking shop, it is usually immovable and not best suited for some everyday tasks. Almost every shop will need some sort of sawhorse. They can be used for a variety of purposes, from supporting long lengths of timber as it is cut, to providing additional support on the infeed and outfeed of a table saw. With the addition of a sheet of plywood, sawhorses make a handy low bench to assemble your latest creation as it is being put together or finished.

To be effective, sawhorses should be easy to make, yet sturdy in use. If they can be folded or disassembled for storage, so much the better. The two designs shown here are simple to build. The first can be built from a few offcuts, folds flat when not needed and is very rigid. Although you could build it with a rope to keep the legs apart, this is not as good as the collapsible stretcher, which keeps the legs apart and allows the horse to be moved around the shop without folding up and trapping the fingers.

The second design is even simpler. Made from just three bits of plywood, it requires no glue or fastenings of any sort. It can be knocked apart in an instant when not needed, saving space in the small workshop. You could even drill a few holes in it and hang it on the wall. I have made both models 24" high for sawing lumber, and the cutting list reflects this. However, you could make them any height by altering the length of the legs to suit yourself.

Although it looks like there is a lot of bevel cutting, all the bevels are the same, so once the sliding bevel is set, do not alter it until the job is finished. A miter saw makes fast work of the cutting, but cutting them by hand is just as good, even if it takes a little longer.

SAWHORSE #1

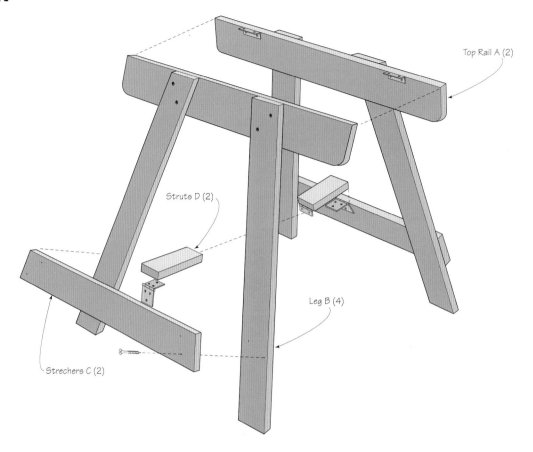

Top Rail A (2)

Struts D (2)

Strechers C (2)

Leg B (4)

SAWHORSE #2

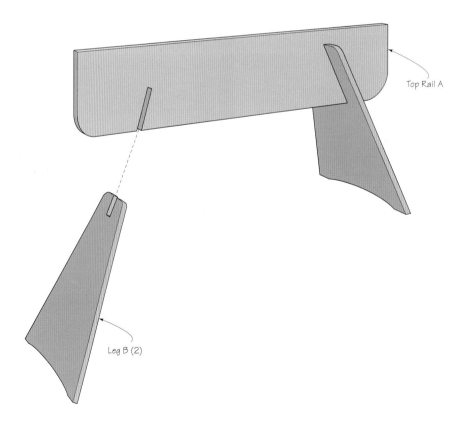

Top Rail A

Leg B (2)

Sawhorse #1 — inches (millimeters)

REFERENCE	QUANTITY	PART	STOCK	THICKNESS	(mm)	WIDTH	(mm)	LENGTH	(mm)	COMMENTS
A	2	rails	pine	1	(25)	$3^{1}/_{2}$	(89)	24	(610)	
B	4	legs	pine	1	(25)	3	(76)	$24^{1}/_{2}$	(623)	
C	2	stretchers	pine	1	(25)	3	(76)	$20^{1}/_{4}$	(514)	
D	1	strut	pine	1	(25)	2	(51)	$11^{1}/_{2}$	(292)	cut in half

Sawhorse #2 — inches (millimeters)

REFERENCE	QUANTITY	PART	STOCK	THICKNESS	(mm)	WIDTH	(mm)	LENGTH	(mm)	COMMENTS
A	1	rail	plywood	$^{3}/_{4}$	(19)	10	(254)	48	(1219)	
B	2	legs	plywood	$^{3}/_{4}$	(19)	16	(406)	23	(584)	

HARDWARE

    Wood glue
16 $1^{1}/_{2}$" (38mm) No. 8 screws
2 3" (76mm) Hinges
3 $1^{1}/_{2}$" (38mm) Back-flap hinges
1 $1^{1}/_{2}$" (38mm) Hinge

SAWHORSE #1

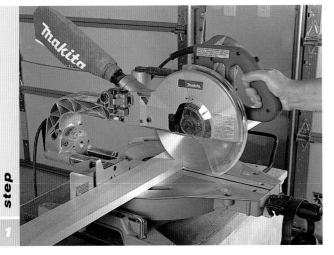

step 1

Start by cutting all the material to length. The rails are cut at right angles, but all the other parts are cut at a 15° angle. You may find it helpful to cut all the legs slightly long, mark the bevels and then recut.

step 2

Set the sliding bevel to 75°. Measure in 6" from each end of the rail and draw a line sloping outward from this mark.

Round off the bottom corners of the rail on the disc sander. Alternatively, cut a small bevel.

Plane a bevel along the length of the rails. This should be only about two-thirds the total width of the rail's width. The remaining flat prevents the knuckle of the hinge from spoiling any work that may be placed on top later.

Check the planed bevel by sighting down the lumber. A beam of light is easy to spot if the bevel is incorrect.

Glue and screw the legs to the rails. Align the outside of the legs with the splayed pencil marks on the rails, making sure that the top of the leg does not project higher than the rail's top edge.

step 7

Fit the stretcher to the outside faces of the legs, keeping the ends flush with the outside edges of the legs.

step 8

Lay the two face frames outward on the bench and fit the 3" hinges 3" in from the ends. A clamp helps to hold the frames tight to one another.

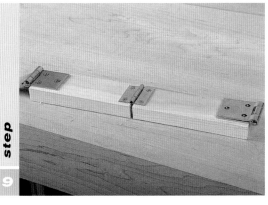

step 9

Cut the strut as shown. Back-flap hinges are fitted at either end, with a standard $1^1/_2$" hinge in the center. Keep the joint open by $^3/_{16}$".

step 10

Fit the strut to the inside of the stretchers. Ensure that it is equally spaced from either end. Remove all sharp corners with sandpaper or a block plane.

step 1

Start by cutting the components out with the jigsaw. Use a fine blade to avoid tearing the plywood surface.

step 2

Use an offcut to accurately mark the width of the notches.

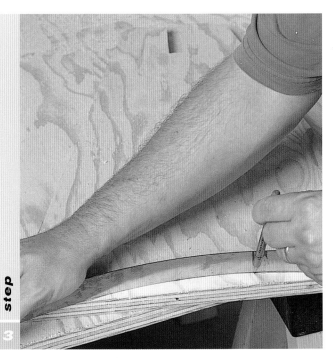

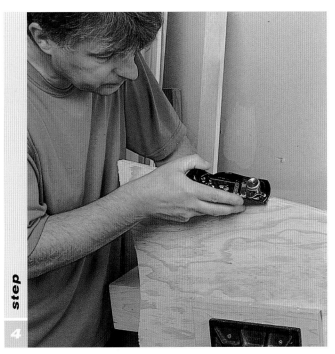

Bend a steel rule and draw around the curve to form the feet. Although you could leave the bottom of the leg straight, it will rock unless the floor is perfectly level.

Remove all sharp corners with a block plane and sandpaper.

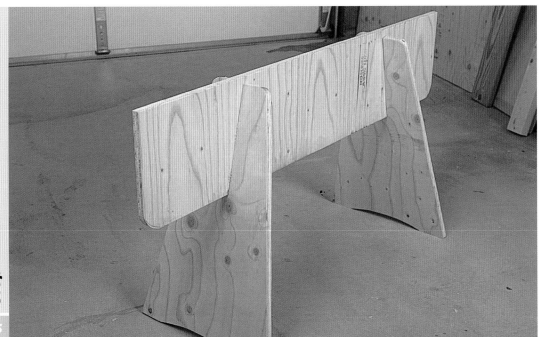

This photo shows the completed sawhorse.

BENCH

This bench is designed to fulfill several functions in the workshop. Primarily it was conceived as a large flat area where jobs could be laid out for assembly, sanding and other work. I have arranged my shop so that the assembly bench is behind me when I am working at the main bench. I then only have to turn around to have the large work surface close at hand.

Medium-density fiberboard (MDF) is used for the top, as it is flat, smooth and inexpensive, so that if it does get damaged, it can be replaced. The flat top is also handy when setting out a job. You can even draw directly on the top, and any pencil marks can be removed when required with an eraser.

Storage below the top can be used for tools and workshop supplies. I put setting and marking tools in the drawers and power tools in the cupboards.

Construction is straightforward and is essentially four face frames screwed together. Making the drawers is probably the hardest part, but you could omit these and install an extra cupboard instead. Rabbeted drawers and doors produce a neat appearance and have the added advantage of preventing dust from entering the cabinet.

When full of tools, the cabinet is very heavy, which adds stability. For a top-of-the-line job, you could exchange the MDF for a solid lumber top, but this would greatly increase the cost.

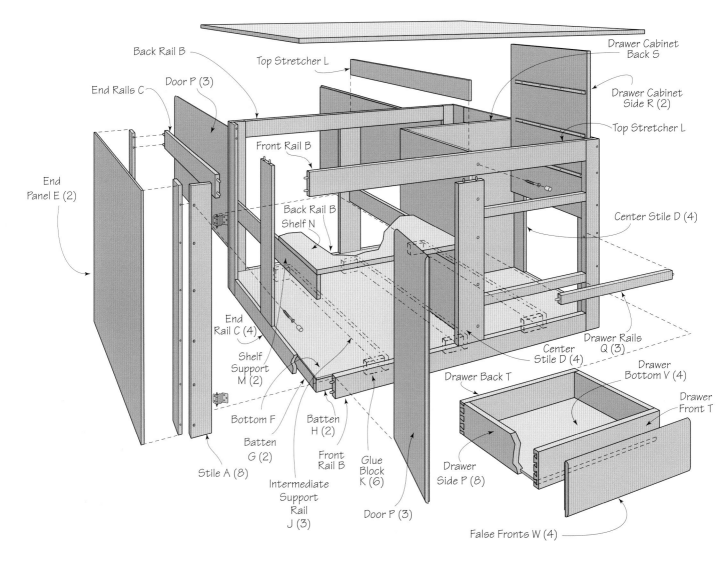

Back Rail B

Door P (3)

End Rails C

Top Stretcher L

Drawer Cabinet Back S

Drawer Cabinet Side R (2)

Top Stretcher L

Front Rail B

End Panel E (2)

Back Rail B

Shelf N

Center Stile D (4)

End Rail C (4)

Shelf Support M (2)

Drawer Rails Q (3)

Center Stile D (4)

Drawer Bottom V (4)

Bottom F

Batten H (2)

Drawer Back T

Drawer Front T

Stile A (8)

Batten G (2)

Front Rail B

Glue Block K (6)

Drawer Side P (8)

Intermediate Support Rail J (3)

Door P (3)

False Fronts W (4)

inches (millimeters)

REFERENCE	QUANTITY	PART	STOCK	THICKNESS	(mm)	WIDTH	(mm)	LENGTH	(mm)	COMMENTS
A	8	stiles	pine	³/₄	(19)	3¹/₂	(89)	34¹/₂	(877)	
B	4	front and back rails	pine	³/₄	(19)	3¹/₂	(89)	52³/₄	(1339)	
C	4	end rails	pine	³/₄	(19)	3¹/₂	(89)	37³/₄	(959)	
D	4	center stiles	pine	³/₄	(19)	5¹/₂	(140)	27⁷/₈	(708)	
E	2	end panels	hardboard	¹/₄	(6)	34¹/₂	(877)	44³/₄	(1137)	
F	1	bottom	hardboard	¹/₄	(6)	43³/₄	(1111)	57³/₄	(1467)	
G	2	battens	pine	³/₄	(19)	2¹/₂	(64)	43¹/₄	(1099)	
H	2	battens	pine	³/₄	(19)	2¹/₂	(64)	57³/₄	(1467)	
J	3	intermediate support rails	pine	³/₄	(19)	3	(76)	43¹/₄	(1098)	relieve undersides
K	6	glue blocks	pine	³/₄	(19)	1¹/₂	(38)	3	(76)	
L	1	top stretcher	pine	³/₄	(19)	3¹/₂	(89)	44³/₄	(1137)	
M	2	shelf supports	pine	³/₄	(19)	3¹/₂	(89)	44³/₄	(1137)	
N	1	shelf	particleboard	³/₄	(19)	30³/₄	(781)	44³/₄	(1137)	
P	3	doors	MDF	³/₄	(19)	24³/₈	(619)	28¹/₄	(718)	
Q	3	drawer rails	pine	³/₄	(19)	1¹/₂	(38)	23⁵/₈	(600)	
R	2	drawer cabinet sides	plywood	³/₄	(19)	20	(508)	31	(787)	
S	1	drawer cabinet back	plywood	³/₄	(19)	23⁵/₈	(600)	31	(787)	
Drawers										
T	8	fronts and backs	pine	³/₄	(19)	4¹/₂	(115)	22¹/₂	(572)	dovetail joints
U	8	sides	pine	³/₄	(19)	4¹/₂	(115)	18	(457)	dovetail joints
V	4	bottoms	hardboard	¹/₄	(6)	21¹/₂	(546)	17³/₄	(451)	
W	4	false fronts	MDF	³/₄	(19)	6³/₄	(171)	24³/₈	(619))	

HARDWARE

	Wood glue
3 pairs	Offset hinges
3	Magnetic catches
4 pairs	18" (457mm) European drawer slides
7	3¹/₂" (89mm) Handles
	³/₄" (19mm) Nails
	⁵/₁₆" (8mm) Dowels
	1¹/₂" (38mm) No. 8 screws
	Metal angle plates

step 1

This bench has a lot of components made from the same type of lumber. Mark the ends of each stack with chalk so that you can easily identify each part. This avoids mistakes and aids assembly.

Start by setting out all the joints for the face frames. There are several ways that you can join the parts together. You can either use biscuits or use dowels as I did. Mortise-and-tenon joints would be a good method, too, but you will have to allow extra material on the ends of the rails and stiles for the tenon length. By clamping all the stiles together, you can save time and increase accuracy by marking out all the shoulder lines at the same time.

After setting out the centers for the dowels (you will need two in each joint), drill the holes to accept $5/16$" dowels. To avoid problems, take care that the register mark on the jig is perfectly aligned with your marks.

Glue up all four frames. Assemble the center stile into the top and bottom rails before gluing on the rest of the stiles. Be sure to attach the three drawer rails to the center stile before attaching the outside stiles to the front panel.

Before the glue sets, it is important to make sure that the frames are square. Measure the frame at the diagonals using a stick or tape measure.

Use a thin batten to measure each of the inside diagonals in turn, putting a pencil mark exactly in line with the corner. If the marks are exactly the same, then the frame is square. If they are not, as shown here, squeeze in the corners across the longer dimension, thus splitting the distance, and the frame will then be square.

Glue and screw the battens that support the bottom to the insides of the frames. Keep them back from each end to allow for the thickness of the adjoining frame. Use an offcut as a spacer, so that when the bottom is finally fitted, it will end up flush with the inside edges of the face frames.

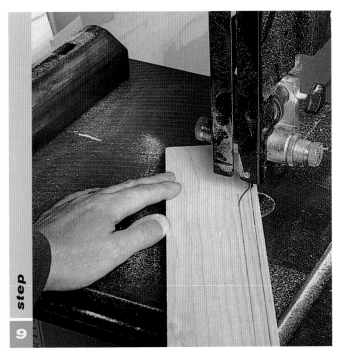

Using ³/₄" nails and glue, attach the hardboard panels to the outside faces of the end frames. Use a nail set to punch the nail heads just below the surface of the hardboard panels.

The bottom is supported on intermediate support rails. A relieving cut, which starts and finishes 3" from each end, will clear any high spots in the floor. I cut these on the band saw, but a jigsaw is just as good.

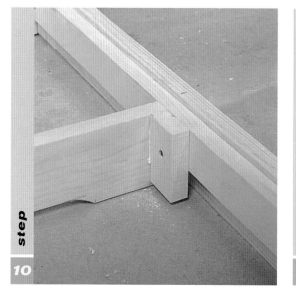

The three intermediate supports are glued and screwed to the inside of the frames. Glue blocks provide support. Note that the tops of the support rail and glue block do not protrude above the base cleat.

Build the plywood drawer box that supports the drawer slides, and glue and screw this into place, noting that the inside of the box aligns with the inside of the face frame.

The particleboard shelf is supported on shelf supports, which are simply screwed to the inside of the face frame and the side of the drawer box. Install the top stretcher.

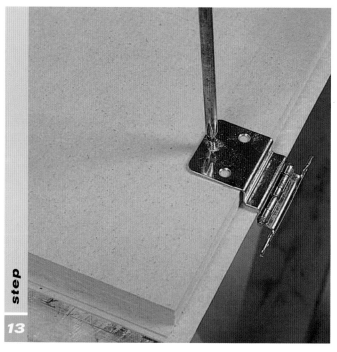

Use offset hinges designed for rabbeted doors. Fit them 3" up and down from the edges. Standard hinges will not work, as the door would bind on the rabbet and prevent it from opening correctly. Buy the hinges before you cut the rabbets, as the depth and width of the rabbet is determined by the hinge.

The drawers are dovetailed for strength. A dovetail jig makes short work of this task, but you can cut them by hand; it just takes a little longer.

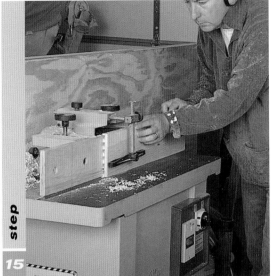

With the dovetailing complete, run the groove for the drawer bottom. It is easy to make a mistake with so many sections of drawer, so be careful and mark each inside face to avoid errors.

After cutting the bottoms, assemble the drawers. If you have cut the joints well, then clamps will not be required. Tap them together after applying the glue. Use a piece of scrap to prevent damage to the drawer side.

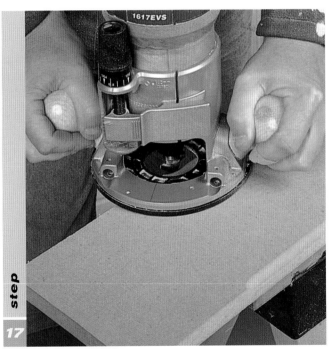

The false fronts are made of MDF. Round over the edges with a bearing-guided cutter in the router.

Fit the drawer slides to the inside of the drawer box. Follow the instructions that come with your particular slides, as they can vary from manufacturer to manufacturer. Note, however, that the front edge of the drawer slide is set in from the front edge the depth of the rabbet on the false front.

A detail of the completed drawer shows the relationship between drawer, drawer slide and false front.

Install metal angle plates at each corner to hold the bench top in place.

Finally, fit the handles of your choice.

USING SCREWS

Everywhere in this book you will see projects that are screwed together, and this assembly bench is no exception. While you could simply glue and screw, countersinking the screw heads, this looks shoddy and unprofessional. You can avoid the unsightly look of the screws by sinking the screws below the surface. Instead of using a countersink, use a $^3/_8$" brad-point drill bit. Fit a wooden sleeve over the drill so that the depth is limited to no more than $^3/_8$" deep. Drill this hole first, followed by the pilot hole for the screw threads.

After driving the screw, glue in a plug. You can either make these yourself with a plug cutter in the drill press or buy them ready-made. When the glue is dry, use a sharp chisel and pare down the protruding plug until it is flush with the surrounding surface. Finally, after sanding, the plug will all but disappear into the surrounding surface.

shaving HORSE

Nobody quite knows the origins of the shaving horse, but it seems likely that it was developed by English chairmakers sometime in the 15th century. But whatever and wherever it came from, there can be no denying the shaving horse's usefulness.

Used by chairmakers for shaving chair parts, they were traditionally made from whatever materials were locally available. Woodworkers would make these in the forest to shape chair parts cut from green or unseasoned wood. My design uses plywood and sections of seasoned timber to make a shaving horse that will last for many years. You can adapt the design, as with just about all the projects in this book, to suit your size and preference, but do not make it too wide as it will be uncomfortable to sit astride for any length of time. None of the parts are complicated to make, and you could use square legs, although this would not look so elegant.

The shaving horse, or shaving brake, as it is sometimes called, is used by sitting astride it. Your feet are placed on the foot pegs, which, in turn, hold the work as you use the drawknife. The wedge is adjusted in or out to suit the thickness of wood being worked on, but you should arrange it so that the end of the workpiece is in line with your belly button. Too low and you could catch your legs with the drawknife; too high and your arms will tire quickly.

The cost of this bench is likely to be minimal, as it could be made from offcuts that you already have in the workshop. I used poplar for the legs, which is stable and turns well, but use whatever you have. Avoid pine for the pivot, which tends to wear, causing the brake to wobble and not work as well.

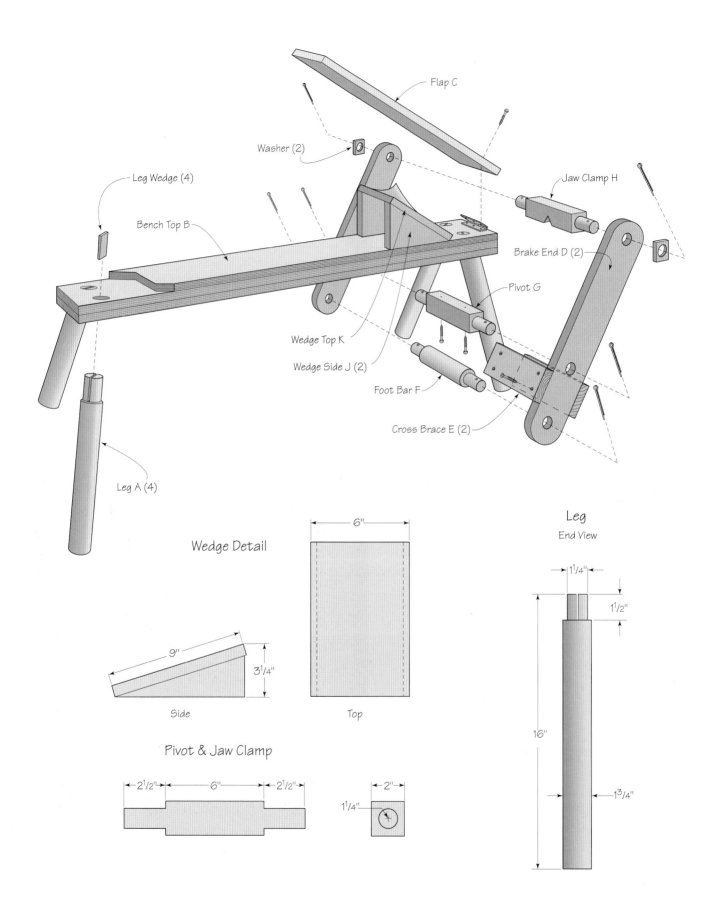

Flap C

Washer (2)

Jaw Clamp H

Leg Wedge (4)

Bench Top B

Brake End D (2)

Pivot G

Wedge Top K

Wedge Side J (2)

Foot Bar F

Cross Brace E (2)

Leg A (4)

Wedge Detail

6"

Leg
End View

1¹/4"

1¹/2"

9"

3¹/4"

Side

Top

16"

1³/4"

Pivot & Jaw Clamp

2¹/2" 6" 2¹/2"

2"

1¹/4"

inches (millimeters)

REFERENCE	QUANTITY	PART	STOCK	THICKNESS	(mm)	WIDTH	(mm)	LENGTH	(mm)	COMMENTS
A	4	legs	poplar	2	(51)	2	(51)	16	(406)	turned to 1³/₄" (45mm) diameter
B	3	bench tops	plywood	³/₄	(19)	6	(152)	52	(1320)	cut one piece ¹/₂" (13mm) oversize
C	1	flap	plywood	³/₄	(19)	6	(152)	21	(533)	
D	2	brake ends	plywood	³/₄	(19)	3	(76)	22	(559)	
E	2	cross braces	plywood	³/₄	(19)	3	(76)	7¹/₂	(191)	
F	1	foot bar	poplar	2	(51)	2	(51)	16	(406)	
G	1	pivot	poplar	2	(51)	2	(51)	11	(279)	ends turned only
H	1	jaw clamp	maple	2	(51)	2	(51)	11	(279)	ends turned only
J	2	wedge sides	plywood	³/₄	(19)	3¹/₄	(82)	8	(203)	triangular — see drawing
K	1	wedge top	plywood	³/₄	(19)	6	(152)	9	(229)	
L	2	washers	hardboard	¹/₄	(6)	2	(51)	2	(51)	
M	4	leg wedges	poplar							cut to fit tapered leg slots

HARDWARE

Wood glue
2 3" (76mm) Hinges
1¹/₂" (38mm) No. 8 screws
2 3" (76mm) Cotter pins
5¹/₂" × 11" Piece of 80-grit sandpaper

Begin by cutting out all the plywood parts. I used ³/₄"-thick plywood, but you can use ¹/₂" because you will be laminating three layers for the bench top. An alternative would be to use solid lumber, but plywood is more stable and less likely to twist or otherwise distort.

Set aside the oversize bench top piece to laminate later. Glue together the bottom two laminations for the bench top with a good-quality wood glue. Spread the adhesive to cover the entire surface.

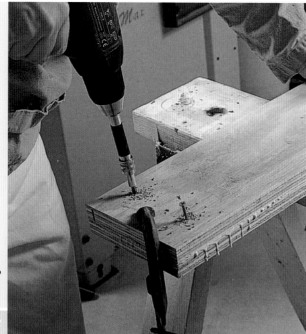

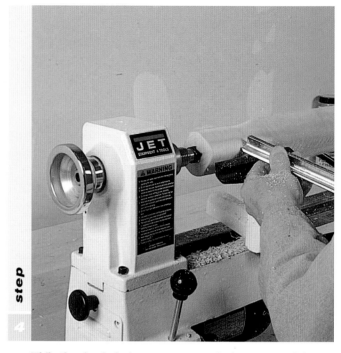

Ensure that the edges are aligned with each other and place a couple of clamps on either end to hold the pieces together while you drive a few screws. Make sure that any screws near the ends are not placed anywhere near where you will drill a hole for the legs. If you come in no more than 2" from each end, the drill bit will clear any screw easily.

While the glue is drying, you can turn the legs. Turn each leg from a 2" square blank. Turn them down to round before turning a tenon on the ends to suit the drill that you will be using for the leg mortises. Refer to the drawing for the dimensions I used. You could make the legs more ornate than I have shown, but remember, this is a workbench, not a Chippendale chair.

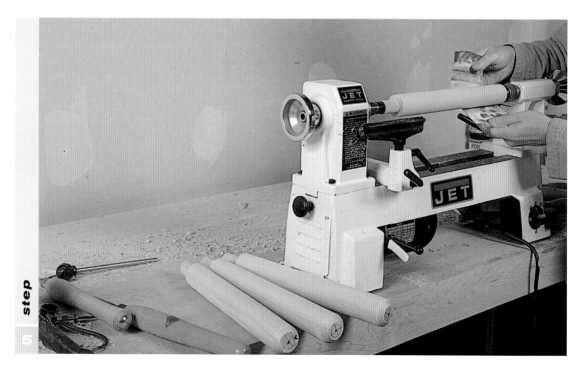

When you have turned each leg to size, sand it with 120-grit paper while it is still on the lathe. Make sure that the tool rest is well out of the way to avoid catching your fingers.

Make a small V-shaped cut in each of the leg tenons with a tenon saw. Taper them from about $^1/_8$" to nothing to suit a small wedge.

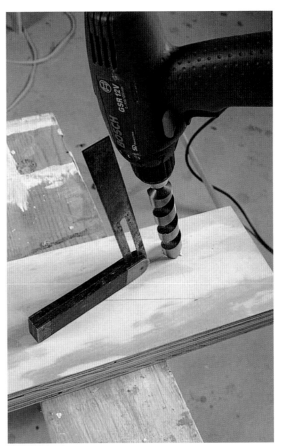

Drill the holes in the bench top to suit the leg tenons. My holes are $1^1/_4$" diameter. You should make the tenons on the leg tops to push-fit into the holes. Note that the photo shows the holes being drilled down through the bench top. To add stability, the legs are splayed out at an 18° angle. Use a sliding bevel as a guide alongside the drill to align the holes correctly.

With all the holes drilled, put glue on the leg tenons and push them into the holes. Cut some small leg wedges, and after running a little glue into the cutouts in the top of the legs, knock in the wedges to lock the legs tight.

After the glue has set, cut the wedges flush with the bench top. A fine, flexible saw is ideal for this.

With the wedges trimmed back, the top lamination can be glued in place. I prefer not to use any screws, which may catch on clothing later, as you will be sitting astride this bench. Instead, use lots of clamps to hold the bits together until the glue sets. I cut the top lamination 1/2" oversize and trimmed off the excess with a trimming cutter in the router later.

Fit the flap to one end of the bench top using two 3" hinges. Either end will do, as the top is symmetrical at this time.

The pivot to the brake is screwed to the underside of the bench top with its center line 15" from the same end as the hinges were fitted. Note that the center section of the pivot is left square. Only the ends that project out beyond the bench edges are turned to $1^{1}/_{4}$" in diameter.

After drilling the three $1^{1}/_{4}$"-diameter holes into each of the two brake ends (see illustration for details), round off the sharp corners on the disc sander. If you do not have a disc sander, round them over with some 80-grit paper wrapped around a block.

Cut a small 90° V into the jaw clamp. Although not absolutely essential, this makes holding small and turned parts much easier and stops them sliding about.

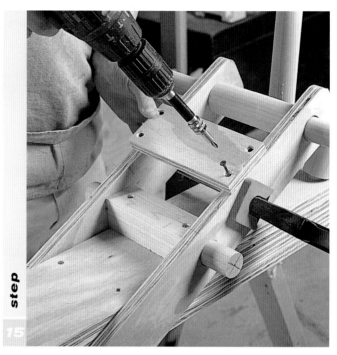

Assemble all the parts of the brakes onto the pivot, noting that no parts are glued save for the two plywood cross braces, which lend strength and support to the assembly just above the foot bar. When gluing and screwing on these cross braces, make sure that one is slightly higher than the other. If they are directly opposite one another, the screws might hit each other, weakening the brake.

Slip a hardboard washer on one end of the jaw clamp, and using a $^3/_{32}$" drill bit, bore through the center of the bar, keeping the drill tight to the washer. Repeat the process for the other side.

step 17

Slide the cotter pins in on each side and bend the tails around to make sure that the pin cannot slide out when the brake is in use.

step 18

The final job is to make the wedge by gluing and screwing the top to the sides.

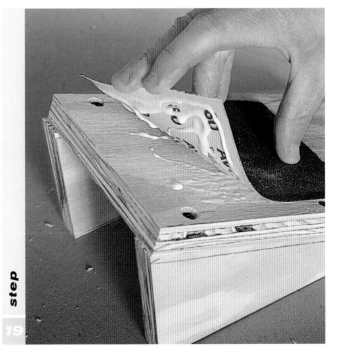

step 19

To prevent the wedge slipping, use a piece of 80-grit sandpaper glued to the top surface. Spread on some wood glue, press down the paper and allow it to dry.

traditional english

SAWHORSE

More years ago than I care to remember, I spent a summer working on a building site in London. Just about all the carpenters had at least a couple of these sawhorses that they used for everything; in essence, this was their workbench. They used them to hold doors while they trimmed the ends, laid sheet material on them while they cut it to size and, with the addition of a couple of 10"-wide boards, used them as a scaffolding while attaching drywall to a ceiling.

Strong and sturdy, the splayed legs give excellent support without tipping, and allow the sawhorses to be stacked one on top of another for storage. Although it may look like an easy project to make, it can trip you up, as the laying out needs care.

The legs splay in two directions, and it is this feature that makes the sawhorse so stable. Unfortunately, it is all too easy to mark out the legs incorrectly. Remember that they are right- and left-handed. Once the sliding bevel is set, it should not be altered until the sawhorse is completely laid out. Study the drawing and the step-by-step photos before you start, as this will pay dividends in speeding up the work.

DETAIL AT TOP OF LEGS

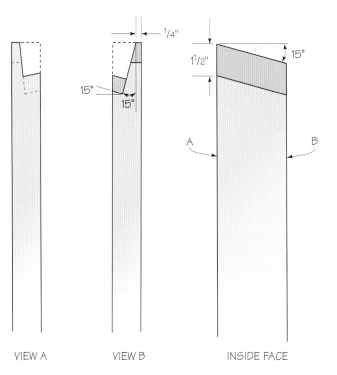

VIEW A   VIEW B   INSIDE FACE

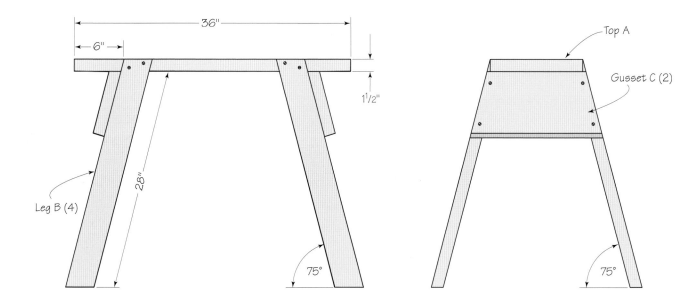

inches (millimeters)

REFERENCE	QUANTITY	PART	STOCK	THICKNESS	(mm)	WIDTH	(mm)	LENGTH	(mm)	COMMENTS
A	1	top	pine	1½	(38)	5½	(140)	36	(914)	
B	4	legs	pine	1½	(38)	3½	(89)	28	(711)	bevel-cut both ends
C	2	gussets	plywood	½	(13)	8	(203)	17	(432)	

HARDWARE

Wood glue
8 1½" (38mm) No. 8 screws
8 2" (51mm) No. 10 screws

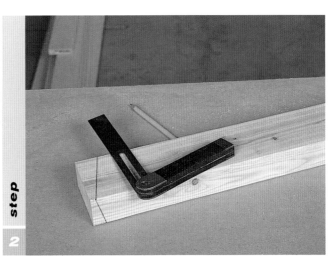

From the high point on the face, draw a line as shown. Once again, do the same thing on the other end of the leg. You will see from the marks that this is simply a compound miter, but marking them avoids confusion.

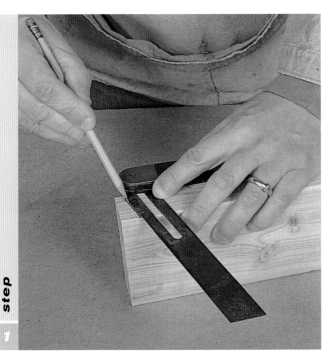

step 1

Before you mark out the joints on the top of the legs, it is necessary to bevel-cut the legs to length. To do this, set the sliding bevel to 15° and mark a line across the face at one end as shown. Then slide the stock of the bevel down to the other end of the leg and mark a second line parallel to the first one.

step 3

Bevel-cut all the legs to length. A sliding miter saw makes this easy if the head can be tilted. Set both the head and the table at 15° and cut the legs to the pencil marks. If you lack a compound miter saw, then cut all the ends with a sharp hand-saw. It is possible to cut the legs on the band saw if you can tilt the table.

step 4

step 5

Now, mark the joints on the top of the legs. For the first leg, draw a line ¹/₂" in, and parallel to, the low edge across the top of the leg. Then, using the previously set sliding bevel, place the stock on the top of the leg and scribe a line as shown on both edges of the leg. (I have taken the bevel off in the picture so you can see how it is done.)

Measure 2" down these lines from the top of the leg, and at right angles to each line, scribe another line across to the edge. Join these two new lines across the inside face of the legs with the sliding bevel; you will see that this line is parallel to the top cut on the leg. Mark the waste to avoid cutting out the wrong bit.

step 6

step 7

Cut out the waste either with a band saw with the table tilted, as I did, or with a handsaw. After cutting this first joint, mark and cut the other three, remembering that one of the others is the same as the one that you have just cut, and the other two face the opposite direction.

If you cut the joints by hand, clean up any roughness in the mating surfaces with a sharp chisel to ensure that the final joint will fit together snugly.

Select which side of the top will be the top surface of the saw-horse, and with this side facing you, measure 6" in from each end. With the sliding bevel sloping outward, draw a line on the edge of the top. Use a scrap of timber the same width as the leg, and with one edge on the inside of the sloping line, draw the second line. Cut along these lines to a depth of $^{1}/_{2}$". Turn over the top and repeat on the other edge.

With the router fitted with a straight cutter, adjusted to a depth of $^{1}/_{2}$", rout out the waste between the cut lines.

Glue and screw the legs to the top using a couple of 2" No. 10 screws on each leg, so that they pull the joint tight. Make sure that the shoulder is tight against the underside of the top.

The final step is to glue and screw the gussets for each pair of legs, using $1^{1}/_{2}$" No. 8 screws. These gussets prevent the legs from spreading and add greatly to the strength. Make these a little oversize and trim them flush with the legs after fitting.

traditional

WORKBENCH

When I moved to this country from England, I had to leave my old bench and most of my machine tools behind. Although I had plenty of tools, I had nowhere to do any woodworking in my new home in Connecticut. What I needed was a bench, and I wanted it now.

The bench had to be solid and able to stand up to years of wear and tear. I also wanted a flat top that I could use for gluing up projects without having them fall into a tool tray. Also, I would eventually be moving my workshop from the garage to the basement, and the bench would have to be disassembled to enable me to get it down through the basement door.

After a seemingly endless amount of measuring and sketching I came up with this design, which produces the traditional workbench in a rather unconventional way: The mortises and tenons are built rather than cut. I have had this bench for some time now, and it has proved to be all that I had hoped. I find the size right for me, but it would be simple to make it longer. Simply increase the length of the rails and lumber for the top.

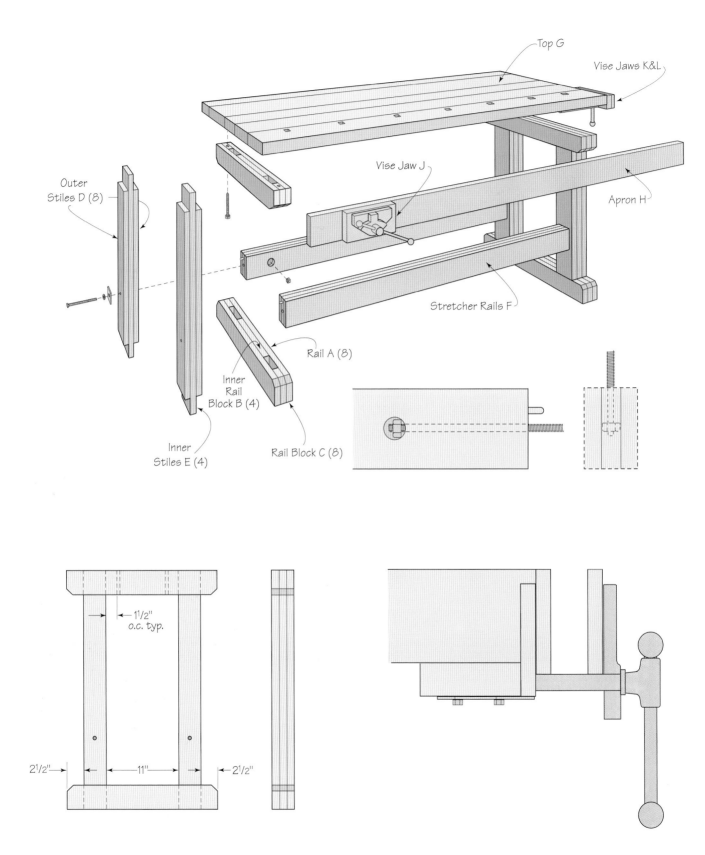

Top G

Vise Jaws K&L

Outer
Stiles D (8)

Vise Jaw J

Apron H

Stretcher Rails F

Rail A (8)

Inner
Rail
Block B (4)

Inner
Stiles E (4)

Rail Block C (8)

1¹/2"
o.c. typ.

2¹/2"   11"   2¹/2"

inches (millimeters)

REFERENCE	QUANTITY	PART	STOCK	THICKNESS	(mm)	WIDTH	(mm)	LENGTH	(mm)	COMMENTS
Frame										
A	4	top outer rails	poplar	7/8	(22)	3 1/2	(89)	23	(584)	
B	4	top inner rails	poplar	7/8	(22)	3 1/2	(89)	11	(279)	
C	8	top inner rail blocks	poplar	7/8	(22)	3 1/2	(89)	2 1/2	(64)	
D	4	foot outer rails	poplar	7/8	(22)	3 1/2	(89)	23	(584)	
E	4	foot inner rails	poplar	7/8	(22)	3 1/2	(89)	11	(279)	
F	4	foot inner rail blocks	poplar	7/8	(22)	3 1/2	(89)	2 1/2	(64)	
G	8	outer stiles	poplar	7/8	(22)	3 1/2	(89)	28	(711)	
H	4	inner stiles	poplar	7/8	(22)	3 1/2	(89)	35	(889)	
J	6	stretcher rails	poplar	7/8	(22)	3 1/2	(89)	74	(1880)	
Bench top										
K	1	top	maple	2	(51)	30	(762)	85	(2159)	make up from narrow boards
L	1	apron	maple	1	(25)	4	(102)	85	(2159)	
M	1	main vise jaw	maple	1	(25)	4	(102)	10	(254)	
N	1	tail vise inner jaw	maple	1	(25)	3	(76)	9	(229)	alter to suit vise
P	1	tail vise outer jaw	maple	2	(51)	3	(76)	9	(229)	

You will also need approximately 2 1/2' (762mm) of maple for the packing blocks under the bench top for both vises. The actual measurement depends on the vise being fitted.

HARDWARE

Wood glue
4   3/8" dia. (10mm dia.) × 36" (914mm) Threaded rods
4   3/8" (10mm) Washers
8   3/8" (10mm) Nuts
4   1/4" (6mm) Brass pins or 1/4"-dia. × 1 1/2"(6mm × 38mm) dowels
Main and tail vise
2   Bench dogs (see suppliers list)
4   3/8" × 4 1/2" (115mm) Lag screws
Plywood splines
No.6 × 1 1/4" (32mm) Screws

BUILDING THE FRAME

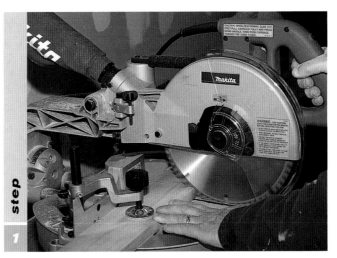

step 1

Cut all the material to length following the cutting list, but do not cut the inner laminations for the rails yet. As the mortises are formed within the inner laminations of the frame, accuracy is vital to avoid sloppy joints. Use the best material for the outer laminations, saving any that has knots or other defects for the inner pieces.

Select one of the outer laminations of the top rails, and on the inside face, square a line across, 3" in from each end. Continue this mark onto each edge of the board, but do not square right across; halfway is ideal.

Using a scrap from the frame material, place this along the tick marks on the edge of the board, and mark the width of the mortises.

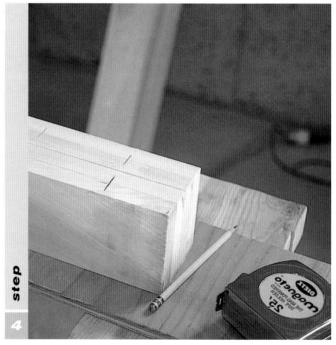

You can see in this view how the marking should look at this point. Measure the distance between the inner marks and cut the inner laminations to this dimension.

Before gluing up the rails, do a dry run. Pay special attention to the width of the mortise. Do not worry if the rail blocks are slightly too long, as they can be trimmed once the glue has set.

Glue up the four rails: the two top rails and the two foot rails. Screws are not necessary for the strength of the rails, but the inner laminations tend to slide about, so put in a couple of $1^{1}/_{4}$" screws to hold them in place before you add the other outer lamination. Make sure that the ends of the wood are accurately aligned with the marks or the tenons will be a poor fit.

Clamp on the outer lamination. Use plenty of clamps but do not use screws, which would spoil the look of the rail.

When the adhesive is completely dry, remove the clamps and clean up the rails with a hand plane. Clean up only the inside edges; you can do the others later, once the complete frame has been finished.

On the foot rails, take off the top corners with a power miter saw. Measure in from the corner $3/4$" and cut the corner at a 45° angle.

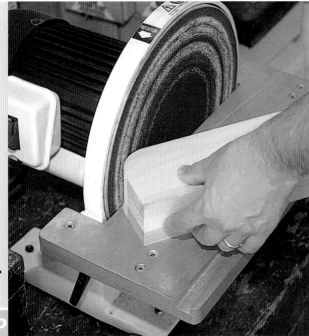

step 10

On the top rails you could do the same or, as I did, round off the corner on the disc sander. This gives the rails a pleasing shape and denotes which is the top rail and which is the foot rail.

step 11

Glue up the stiles, then glue up the frames. Clamp them together and use a pinch rod to check the diagonals. Discrepancy is indicative of an out-of-square frame. Move the clamps and recheck.

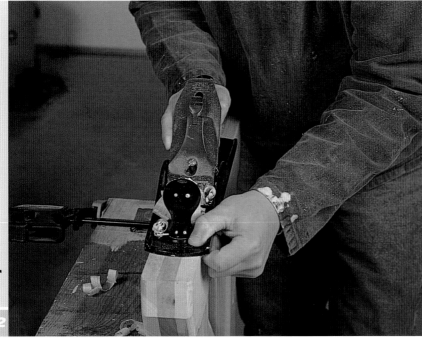

step 12

Leave the frames flat overnight to allow the glue plenty of time to set. Then plane off the protruding tenons with a sharp plane. Lay the frames flat and clean up the faces before sanding for final finish.

The stretcher rails are simple to make, but the key is getting the threaded rod positioned correctly. Refer to the stretcher rail detail drawing, and you can also see here how all the parts correlate to one another. On the center line of the middle lamination, measure in 6" from each end and bore a 1"-diameter hole. Drill a $^7/_{16}$"-diameter clearance hole into the end for the threaded rod so that the rod will come out into the center of the large hole. Drop a nut into the large hole with a flat resting on the outer lamination. Insert the rod through the clearance hole and screw it into the nut until at least three threads are visible through the other side. Glue on the other lamination, making sure the ends are flush. Clamp up and when the glue has dried, clean it up with plane and sandpaper.

Knock in a $^1/_4$"-diameter brass pin 1" up from the bottom of the rail. This is merely to prevent the rail from turning once the bench is assembled. If you do not have of any of these pins, then use a $^1/_4$" dowel.

You are now ready to assemble the bench. Feed the threaded rod through the holes in the end frames and push up until the pins make a small indentation on the inside face of the frames. Disassemble and, at the indentation, drill a clearance hole for the pin.

Reassemble the base, sliding large washers and nuts onto each threaded rod. Tighten the nuts with a wrench, but be careful not to overtighten.

Cut off any protruding threaded rod with a hacksaw, leaving at least three threads showing. Remove any burr with a metal file.

Run the edges of the top timbers over the jointer to get the edges as flat and true as possible. They need to be square to the faces, too, so make certain that the fence on your jointer is true to the bed. Take light cuts, sighting down the edge until you are sure that you have the edges as straight as possible with the jointer.

Using the longest plane that you have (I used a No. 8), remove the ripple marks left from the jointer and truly flatten the edges of the timber in preparation for gluing. With a sharp blade in the plane, aim for getting a continuous shaving from one end of the board to the other.

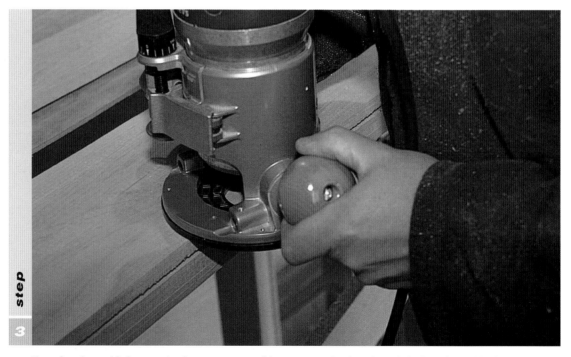

Use a bearing-guided cutter in the router to machine a groove in the edge of the board suitable for a plywood spline. The plywood should be a snug fit but not too tight, or when the glue is applied, it may bind in the slot. An alternative would be to use biscuits, but whichever you choose, work from the face side so that the top will be flush at glue-up.

Before glue-up bore the $^3/_4$"-diameter through-holes for the bench dogs, 4" in from the edge of what will be the front board in the bench top. Use a Forstner bit for a clean hole and set these at 6" centers. Place the last hole at least 18" from the end, or the holes will interfere with the placement of the main vise.

Use plenty of clamps and glue up the top, keeping it flat. Use a straightedge to ensure that the clamps are not cupping the top. If they are, place additional clamps on the bow side to pull the top flat. Provided you were careful in the preparation of the lumber, any discrepancy should be slight.

After leaving the glue to dry overnight, remove the clamps and use a sharp smoothing plane to clean up the top. Plane both down the length and across the diagonal to remove all high spots. Sharpen the plane frequently to prevent tear-out of the bench surface. Finish with light stokes along the grain.

Sand the top. Avoid using a belt sander, which puts ridges in the surface and is too aggressive. Use a random-orbit or finishing sander, starting with 80-grit sandpaper before finishing with 120 grit. Keep the sander moving all the time and do not forget the edges.

If the bench is a little long, trim off the ends to give a neat appearance. Run a jigsaw against a guide, then either plane the end smooth or use a straight cutter in a router to remove the saw marks.

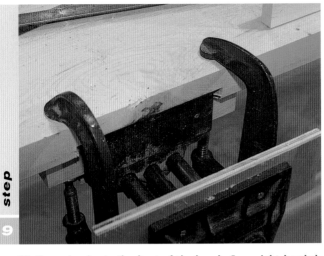

Fit the main vise to the front of the bench. I am right-handed and the vise is mounted about 1' in from the left end. If you are left-handed, you will need to mount the vise the same distance in from the right end of the bench top. Chop into the front of the bench top so that the top of the back jaw is about 1" down from the work surface. You will need a packing block between the vise and the underside of the bench, the thickness of which varies with the bench and the vise during use.

Here is an underside view of the bench. You can see how the packing block sits between the underside of the bench and the vise mounting plate.

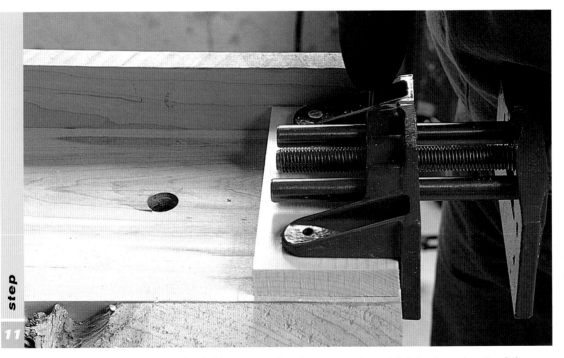

The tail vise is mounted in a similar fashion, except I prefer not to cut a notch into the end grain of the bench for the inner jaw.

The inner jaw is covered by a 1×3 section of timber that is routed out to completely cover the inner metal jaw. To make it safer to machine, make the jaw oversize, then cut it to length after routing.

If you did not bore for the bench dogs before gluing the top together, do it now with the $^{3}/_{4}$" bit in a hand drill. Be certain the drill is vertical. Back up on the underside to prevent breakout.

Here is the completed tail vise with the bench dogs in place. Note that the outer jaw on the vise is thicker than normal because of the hole that is needed to accommodate the moving dog.

Cut a $3/4$" elongated slot $1^1/2$" in from each tenon on the end frames, as clearance holes for the lag screws. This is essential or seasonal movement will pull the bench top and frame apart.

Locate the bench top squarely on the leg assembly and bolt down the top using a suitably sized wrench.

SUPPLIERS

American Tool Companies, Inc.
92 Grant Street
Wilmington, Ohio 45177-0829
937-382-3811
www.americantool.com
Record vises

B&Q
B&Q Head Office
Portswood House
1 Hampshire Corporate Park
Chandlers Ford
Eastleigh
Hampshire
SO53 3YX
023 8025 6256
www.diy.com
Tools, paint, wood, electrical, garden

The Home Depot
Attention: Customer Care
2455 Paces Ferry Road
Atlanta, Georgia 30339
800-553-3199 (U.S.)
800-668-2266 (Canada)
www.homedepot.com
Tools, paint, wood, electrical, garden

Jesada Tools
310 Mears Boulevard
Oldsmar, Florida 34677
800-531-5559
www.jesada.com
Router bits

Lee Valley Tools Ltd.
U.S.:
P.O. Box 1780
Ogdensburg, New York 13669-6780
800-267-8735
Canada:
P.O. Box 6295, Station J
Ottawa, Ontario, Canada K2A 1T4
800-267-8761
www.leevalley.com
Bench dogs and other bench hardware

**Lowe's Home Improvement
Warehouse**
Customer Care
P.O. Box 1111
North Wilkesboro, North Carolina 28656
800-445-6937
www.lowes.com
Tools, paint, wood, electrical, garden

Robert Bosch Tool Corporation
4300 West Peterson Avenue
Chicago, Illinois 60646
877-267-2499
www.boschtools.com
Power tools

Woodcraft
P.O. Box 1686
Parkersburg, West Virginia 26102-1686
800-225-1153
www.woodcraft.com
Woodworking hardware and
accessories

INDEX

THE BEST
WOODWORKING
PROJECTS
COME FROM
POPULAR
WOODWORKING
BOOKS!

These and other Popular Woodworking titles are available from your local bookstore, on-line supplier or by calling 1-800-448-0915.

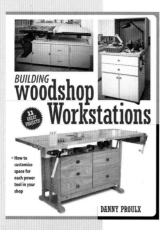

Build the workshop of your dreams! Danny Proulx provides detailed plans and easy-to-follow instructions for building 12 completely self-contained units for every tool and related accessory. Each design ensures that the wrenches, blades, jigs and attachments for all your tools are within arm's reach.

ISBN 1-55870-637-2, paperback, 128 pages, #70585-K

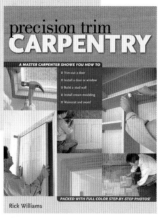

In *Building the Perfect Tool Chest*, Jim Stack shows you how to build 15 stylish yet practical toolboxes tailored to your specific needs. Projects range from elegant rolling cabinets to utilitarian tote boxes. It's an exciting selection that ensures something for every woodworker, no matter what your level of skill.

ISBN 1-55870-650-X, paperback, 128 pages, #70598-K

Here's all the instruction you need to craft professional-level precision trim carpentry. Start-to-finish guidelines and step-by-step photos make any project easy. Want to trim a door? Replace a window? Install wainscot panels? Whatever the job at hand, master carpenter Rick Williams makes sure you have the information you need to do it right.

ISBN 1-55870-636-4, paperback, 128 pages, #70584-K

Plan, design, construct and install your own complete handmade kitchen, from simple cabinets and over-the-sink cupboards to lazy-Susan shelving, stemware storage and more. Danny Proulx's start-to-finish guidelines make it easy. You'll also find practical information on kitchen design, material selection and tool shortcuts.

ISBN 1-55870-676-3, paperback, 128 pages, #70626-K